THE SEVEN RULES OF WALL STREET

CRASH-TESTED INVESTMENT STRATEGIES THAT BEAT THE MARKET

SAM STOVALL

New York   Chicago   San Francisco   Lisbon   London   Madrid
Mexico City   Milan   New Delhi   San Juan   Seoul
Singapore   Sydney   Toronto

1 2 3 4 5 6 7 8 9 0   DOC/DOC   0 1 0 9

ISBN 978-0-07-161517-4
MHID   0-07-161517-2

This publication is designed to provide accurate and authoritative information in regard to the subject matter covered. It is sold with the understanding that neither the author nor the publisher is engaged in rendering legal, accounting, or other professional service. If legal advice or other expert assistance is required, the services of a competent professional person should be sought.

> —*From a Declaration of Principles jointly adopted*
> *by a Committee of the American Bar Association*
> *and a Committee of Publishers and Associations*

I dedicate this book to my best friend, whose warm and wise counsel always encouraged my growth, supported my endeavors, comforted my failures, and acknowledged my accomplishments.

CONTENTS

I have a feeling that when my ship comes in I'll be at the airport.

—Charlie Brown

PREFACE

Don't Miss the Surge After the Slump

From October 9, 2007 through November 20, 2008, the S&P 500 lost 52% of its value. Many investors, as a result, are now repeatedly chanting the line from the Beatles' song "Yesterday" "Suddenly, I'm not half the man I used to be." They are also wondering if they should sell what little they have left and never invest in stocks again. My advice is "Don't be a Charlie Brown." Not because I want you to buy this book, but because: 1) very few people can divine stock market bottoms—I'm not one of them, 2) the beginnings of new bull markets are usually fast and furious, recouping an average of one-third of the entire bear market loss in only 40 days and typically rising 46% in the first year alone, and 3) the rules in this book have frequently outpaced the market's first-year advance with some rules beating the market by a more than 2-to-1 margin.

In other words, I don't want you to miss out on the surge after the slump. I don't want you to be at the airport just as your ship is pulling in. Your ship is the rapid rise in share prices after bear market bottoms that will help your portfolio get back to break-even, typically in a little more than five years. In addition, many of the Rules of Wall Street have historically speeded up this recovery time.

UNPARALLELED UGLINESS

Let's face it. The bear market of 2007–2008 was the perfect storm of popping bubbles—commodities, emerging markets, hedge funds, and real estate. But don't feel too bad about not anticipating this meltdown or the beating suffered by your portfolio. Unless someone's portfolio was either heavily invested in cash or bear-market funds, other people's portfolios probably performed as poorly as yours did.

While the S&P 500 was losing more than 50% of its value, Figure P.1 shows that there was no place to hide. All 10 sectors within the "500" fell in price, with the financials sector tumbling by 74%. In addition, all but three of the 130 industries in the S&P 500 posted declines during this 13-month period. Surprisingly, U.S. equities declined less than did international developed country equities, and emerging markets equities from October 2007 through November 2008.

But you know what? This is the kind of price performance that typically happens in a bear market. Granted, the cause and speed of this bear market was unprecedented. It reached mega-meltdown status by losing more than 40% in

FIGURE P.1

In a Bear Market, There's No Place to Hide

S&P 500 Sector Performances
This Bear and Average Bears: 1946–2008

	% Change	**Average 1946–2002**	
S&P 500 Sectors	**10/9/07–11/20/08**	**% Chg.**	**Rank**
Consumer Staples	−22%	−10%	1
Utilities	−37%	−20%	3
Health Care	−38%	−14%	2
Energy	−44%	−23%	4
Telecommunications Services	−49%	−37%	10
S&P 500/All Industries	−52%	−25%	NA
Information Technology	−53%	−27%	6
Industrials	−55%	−32%	9
Consumer Discretionary	−57%	−31%	8
Materials	−58%	−25%	5
Financial	−74%	−28%	7

Source: Standard & Poor's Equity Research
Past performance is no guarantee of future results.

13 months, rather than the typical 21 months. However, I expect the recovery to be similar to other recoveries from severe bear markets. What's more, I suspect that many of the Rules of Wall Street will record advances in the first year of a new bull market that will far exceed that of the overall market. Why? Because this is just what the market did following the other post-WWII mega-meltdowns of 1973–1974 and 2000–2002.

HISTORY AS VIRTUAL VALIUM

Let's examine bear market recovery times and the relative outperformance by some of the Rules of Wall Street.

This is the 16th bear market since 1929. Its more than 50% decline makes it the worst bear market since 1945, and the third worst since 1929. But when this bear market finally ends, be prepared for a fast and furious partial recovery. Figure P.2 shows that in the first year of a new bull market, the average price rise for the S&P 500 was 46%. What's more, the "500" recovered more than 82% of the prior bear market's loss in that first year. I can't guarantee that the market will respond the same way this time around, but successful investors play the odds—and the odds point to a surge in the first year of a new bull market.

THE RULES "RULE," AS A RULE

In 2008, the Sell in May portfolio beat the S&P 500 by more than 15 percentage points, as investors gravitated toward defensive issues from May through October. But what about the other Rules of Wall Street? How did they fare in the last year of a mega-meltdown and in the first year of a new bull market?

Figure P.3 shows the performance of the S&P 500 and five of the Rules in 1974 and 2002—the last two years of the prior two mega-meltdowns, or bear markets that lost 48%

FIGURE P.2

Bounces Off of the Bear Markets Gone By

	S&P 500 Price Changes and Recovery of Prior Bear Markets in First Year of New Bull Market		
Bull Markets		1st Year S&P 500	Recovery of Prior
Start	**End**	**Change**	**Bear Market**
6/1/1932	7/18/1933	121%	19%
3/14/1935	3/6/1937	81%	158%
3/31/1938	11/9/1938	29%	24%
4/28/1942	5/29/1946	55%	65%
6/13/1949	8/2/1956	42%	100%
10/22/1957	12/12/1961	31%	112%
6/27/1962	2/9/1966	33%	84%
10/7/1966	11/29/1968	33%	115%
5/26/1970	1/11/1973	44%	78%
10/3/1974	11/28/1980	38%	41%
8/12/1982	8/25/1987	58%	157%
12/4/1987	7/16/1990	21%	42%
10/11/1990	3/24/2000	29%	117%
10/9/2002	10/9/2007	34%	35%
Averages		**46%**	**82%**

Source: Standard & Poor's Equity Research
Past performance is no guarantee of future results.

and 49%, respectively. It also shows the performances in 1975 and 2003, the first years of a new bull market following the mega-meltdowns. The Let Your Winners Ride, There's Always a Bull Market Someplace, and As Goes January portfolios for Industries trounced the S&P 500 in the first year of a new bull market. Since 1990, these rules-using sectors also beat the market coming out of mega-bears, as did the No Free Lunch and equally weighted portfolios.

FIGURE P.3

Magnified Movements Following Bear Markets

Performances of "The Rules of Wall Street" in the Last Year of the Mega-Meltdown and First Year of New Bull Market

The Rules of Wall Street	% Changes			
	1974	1975	2002	2003
Let Your Winners Ride				
Industries	−23.9%	35.8%	−11.6%	34.5%
Cap-Weighted Sectors	−	−	−19.9%	22.1%
Equally Weighted Sectors	−	−	−10.1%	27.6%
There's Always a Bull Market Someplace				
Industries	−21.0%	45.1%	−10.0%	41.6%
Cap-Weighted Sectors	−	−	−13.8%	13.6%
Equally Weighted Sectors	−	−	−8.3%	26.0%
As Goes January				
Industries	−19.2%	81.3%	−18.2%	72.9%
Cap-Weighted Sectors	−	−	−21.4%	35.2%
Equally Weighted Sectors	−	−	−16.2%	53.8%
No Free Lunch				
Cap-Weighted Sectors	−	−	−21.9%	27.9%
Equally Weighted Sectors	−	−	−25.5%	44.7%
S&P 500	**−29.7%**	**31.5%**	**−23.4%**	**26.4%**

Source: Standard & Poor's Equity Research.
Past performance is no guarantee of future results.

So what will happen this time around? Will a new bull market emerge in 2009? Will the Rules of Wall Street soar again? No one knows for sure, but I believe that if you stay out of stocks because of the beating you just received, you will likely end up at the airport when your ship finally comes in.

ACKNOWLEDGMENTS

Without the help of Leah Spiro, Kenya Henderson, Daina Penikas, and Gayathri Vinay—my McGraw-Hill editorial and marketing team of superheros—*The Seven Rules of Wall Street* would have ended up being just another vanity book. Their professional guidance and personal efforts, combined with their encouraging and charming demeanors, made the creation of this investment guide a very pleasurable experience.

A man's got to know his limitations.

—DIRTY HARRY

INTRODUCTION

The Key to Investment Success

WHO AM I?

Hello, I'm Sam Stovall, Chief Investment Strategist of Equity Research at Standard & Poor's (S&P). I have been with S&P for 20 years, serving as analyst, publisher, and communicator of S&P's outlooks for the economy, market, sectors, and stocks. I chair our Investment Policy Committee, where I focus on market history and valuations, as well as sector and industry recommendations. I am also a frequent guest on financial TV.

In 1995 and 1996, I authored two editions of *The Standard & Poor's Guide to Sector Investing*, which are now selling online at flatteringly high prices. Today, my weekly articles are found on "Stovall's Sector Watch," a page on www.spoutlook.com, which focuses on market/sector history as well as sector/industry momentum.

Prior to S&P, I was editor-in-chief at Argus Research, an independent investment research firm in New York City. I received an MBA in Finance from New York University and a BA in History/Education from Muhlenberg College, in Allentown, Pennsylvania. Finally, when I wanted to learn how to get my own financial house in order, I became a Certified Financial Planner.

MY BEST ADVICE

Despite all of this formal education, the best bit of investment advice I ever got actually came from the least likely of sources: Clint Eastwood, when he played Dirty Harry in the movie *Magnum Force*. Throughout the film, he repeatedly growled through clenched teeth, "A man's got to know his limitations." That got me thinking. While astute job seekers focus on their strengths, I have concluded that wise investors acknowledge their weaknesses. That way, they avoid becoming their own worst enemy.

With that advice in mind, I began wondering, what are my limitations? Three instantly came to mind. I am:

1. Indecisive
2. Impatient
3. Emotional

All through school, I had a hard time taking multiple-choice tests, because I could always talk myself out of the right answer. Jokingly, I now tell friends that one semester I came home with a report card showing four "Fs" and one

"D." When my father asked, "*What happened*?" I told him I spent too much time on one subject.

When it comes to selecting stocks, I have a similar experience. After I have concluded that an investment choice might succeed, I instantly start thinking of the reasons why it might fail. As a result, I end up becoming frozen by indecision. Does that ever happen to you? Just to indicate how indecisive I can be at times, I recently concluded that my favorite color is plaid.

After finally making an investment decision, I instantly want to see it rise in price, for I definitely didn't have the conviction to buy something today in the expectation that it will prove to be a winner a year or two from now. Well, what did you expect from a guy who gets upset if he misses a slot in a revolving door?

Finally, I am an extremely emotional investor. If I make a decision, and then the price goes against me, I anguish over that decision, probably because I know that so many fundamental variables are pushing and pulling the price every minute of every day. I guess I'm not alone, since fear and greed are the primary motivators of investors in the near-to-intermediate term. What's more, in this age of instant—and overwhelming—information, I have realized that I now experience both fear and greed at the exact same moment.

At this point you are probably wondering why would I want to take advice from this guy if he has limitations that are similar to mine? While I admit that I am indecisive, impatient, and emotional, I never said I was not an opportunist. I never said I wasn't willing to leverage the knowledge of thousands of investors who are probably a lot smarter than me. Therefore, being aware of my weaknesses, I have searched for, and found, market-beating investment techniques that overcome my weaknesses. They stop me from becoming my own worst enemy. As a result, these rules serve as a Marine Corps drill instructor barking: "Don't think, just do what I tell you!"

I believe parents, teachers, and investment advisors all have at least one thing in common: they offer shortcuts to success to their children, students, and clients. That's what I hope to accomplish in this book—to offer shortcuts to investment success by making you aware of these seven crash-tested Rules of Wall Street.

REFINING THE RULES OF THUMB

I have always heard that there is a hint of truth in every rumor. So, I wondered if the same could be said of Wall Street's "rules of thumb." Could I leverage these rules into investment disciplines that beat the Street? I reasoned that there had to be some truth in them, otherwise they would never have been created.

For at least 15 years, I have spoken at the Money Shows—investment symposiums for individual investors—that are held in four cities in the United States: Orlando, Las Vegas, San Francisco, and Washington, D.C. (Please visit www.intershow.com for more information.) Investors attend these symposiums to interact with well-known investment advisors, scoop up dozens of investment newsletters for free, get advice or stock tips, and become educated on investment disciplines or philosophies that they can later use to their own advantage. They pay nothing to attend. The speakers foot the bill through exhibit hall fees.

S&P usually sends three people to each Money Show venue. We typically hold an end-of-show panel discussion, sharing our outlook for the global economy, how we think the stock market will trend in the coming months, which sectors we like and dislike, as well as which stocks to buy, hold, or sell. The organizer's intent is to use S&P as an anchor to keep the attendees around until the very end of the show.

Each of S&P's experts is also asked to give a workshop, explaining a particular investment technique that would be helpful to these individual investors. Over the past several years, I have been refining my workshop "Sector Rotation Strategies Using Old Wall Street Sayings," which validates the old sayings through performance backtesting and then identifies how an investor can develop a market-beating portfolio by employing these sayings or rules of thumb. Not only did this talk become *The Seven Rules of Wall Street*, but one of these rules also became the discipline that I use for investing my own individual retirement account (IRA). I will explain all seven rules so that you may select your personal favorite.

THE COMPOSITION OF THE S&P 500

Before I dive into the Seven Rules of Wall Street, I think I should give you a little bit of background into the Standard & Poor's 500 index (S&P 500), the world's most widely followed benchmark of U.S. large-company, or large-capitalization, stocks. Not surprisingly, there are 500 stocks in this exclusively U.S. large-cap equity index.

There are three types of capitalization benchmarks: large cap, mid cap, and small cap. Each one refers to the size of the typical stock found within the benchmark, or the market that this overall index is attempting to emulate. Capitalization is computed by multiplying the number of common shares outstanding by the share price. For instance, on April 30, 2008, Exxon Mobil Corp. (XOM) was the largest company in the S&P 500 Index. It had a market cap of $499 billion (5.35 billion shares x $93.07 per share).

Typically, a company is called large cap if its capitalization is above $4.0 billion, while a small-cap company is

$1.5 billion or less in size. A mid-cap stock is anything in between. The average market cap of companies in the S&P 500 is $24.13 billion, whereas the average market caps for the S&P MidCap 400 and S&P SmallCap 600 indexes are $2.73 billion and $0.83 billion, respectively.

These 500 companies in the S&P 500 are assembled into 130 industries and 10 sectors. Companies that sell similar products or services are assigned to a particular industry. For instance, Coke and Pepsi make nonalcoholic beverages, and therefore are assigned to the S&P 500 Soft Drinks Industry index.

Industries, on the other hand, which provide similar services and also are affected in like ways by economic events or legislative/regulatory considerations, are assigned to one of 10 sectors. Soft drink companies, as well as brewers, household products, and tobacco companies, are assigned to the S&P Consumer Staples sector index.

In Rule 6, I go into greater detail on the S&P 500 index, as well as the concept of a market-capitalization-weighted index.

Finally, all of the performance data shown in this book reflects price performances, not total returns. In other words, no dividends were included in any calculations. More information about the S&P 500 can be found at www.sandp.com.

S&P WEB SITES

There are four S&P Web sites that will likely be very useful resources for your investment pursuits. One is free, while three have monthly/annual subscription fees.

- www.sandp.com
- www.spoutlook.com
- www.advisorinsight.com
- www.netadvantage.sandp.com

sandp.com

A free site that introduces the visitor to the wide-ranging services offered by Standard & Poor's is www.sandp.com. Specifically, it provides data, commentary, and videos emanating from the Ratings, Indices, Equity Research, Risk Management, Advisory Services, and Data divisions.

An important source of sector and industry information is available free of charge in the "Indices" section. From the left side, just click on the "Equity Indices" tab, select "United States," click on "S&P 500," and then choose "S&P 500 GICS Sector Scorecard," and you'll see return data for the sectors and industries in the S&P 500. If you have difficulty, simply perform a search on "S&P 500 GICS Sector Scorecard," and you'll be directed to the proper page.

The Outlook Online

Standard & Poor's research publication for individual investors is *The Outlook*. This 12-page investment newsletter has been published since the early 1920s. The print publication is produced weekly and costs $298 per year.

The *Outlook Online* edition delivers an electronic version of the newsletter, as well as a variety of screening tools, preconstructed portfolios, and videos. The online version features exclusive investment strategies, penetrating market insights, S&P's highly regarded stock and fund research and tools, and comprehensive investment education from the leader in independent and objective investment research. It also provides a weekly update of the S&P 1500 Sector Scorecard, which shows trailing 12-month price performances for the sectors and industries within the total U.S. stock market benchmark. It is from this scorecard that you can keep track of the leading and lagging sectors, as described in this book. The *Outlook Online* is offered for $19.95 per month, or $200 per year.

Advisor Insight

Standard & Poor's Advisor Insight provides financial advisors with online access to Standard & Poor's renowned investment research and data with tools to stay abreast of the market, deliver investment insights to clients, and grow assets under management.

Primary services include MarketScope, intra-day market commentary, news, and investment research and analysis; stock reports, in-depth S&P research, analysis, and tools on more than 1,500 U.S. and 300 non-U.S. corporations, including qualitative buy, sell, and hold S&P STARS opinions; and commentary, rankings, and recommended weightings of 10 sectors, supported by forecasts and detailed industry survey reports.

Many investors may already have access to S&P research and sector scorecards through their discount- and full-service broker's Web sites. Give them a call to find out.

NetAdvantage

If your broker can't help you tap into S&P's investment recommendations, maybe your library can. NetAdvantage is a comprehensive source of business and investment information, offered to librarians, universities, and other institutional professionals. It provides online access to popular Standard & Poor's research products such as Industry Surveys, Stock Reports, Corporation Records, The Register of Corporations, Directors and Executives, *The Outlook*, and Mutual Fund Reports. Maybe this could be a way to access S&P at no additional cost. I say additional, since you are already paying for your library through local, county, and state taxes.

Now back to the basics.

THE BASICS OF BACKTESTING

To see if an investment approach or discipline is worthwhile, investors need to do their homework by backtesting the results over an extended period of time. In other words, determine how this technique would have performed over many years, incorporated several economic cycles, as well as during bull and bear markets. If an investment rule does not beat "the market," why waste your time and money by racking up huge trading costs and then going through the nightmare of filing your taxes come April? You would have been better off investing in an S&P 500 index fund or exchange-traded fund (ETF) and spending the rest of your time reading a good book.

When analyzing industry performances within a particular rule, I usually started with 1970, since this near 40-year "look back" would incorporate the mega-meltdowns of 1973–1974 and 2000–2002, in which the S&P 500 twice lost nearly 50% of its value, as well as the 1995–1999 period in which the S&P 500 gained more than 20% every year. I wanted to see how these disciplines held up under crisis testing. While Standard & Poor's has industry data going back to the 1940s, we only started distributing sector-level data in 1990. As a result, even though my industry analyses go back nearly 40 years, my sector studies date back to only 1990.

In each of the following chapters I will tell you the steps I took in performing the backtest for each rule, so that you may fully understand the process. At the end of each chapter I will show you—step by step—how to set up your own portfolio, based on that chapter's particular rule.

CONSIDER RETURNS AND FREQUENCIES

Investors should judge their results on two things: the average price advance for the rule versus the S&P 500, as well as the frequency with which the rule beat the overall market. Sure, it's nice to have a rule that beat the "500" by a wide margin, but it might be hard to stick by this rule if it succeeded less than half of the time. Sometimes you'll come across an investment approach that strikes out frequently but hits home runs every so often. I don't know about you, but I'd prefer to exchange some long-term price advantage for an increase in consistency of outperformance.

I think an investment rule is worthwhile if it offers at least 300 basis points of annual outperformance (meaning its average price change was better than the S&P 500's by at least 3 percentage points per year) and its frequency of beating the S&P 500 is at least 67% (it beats the market in two out of every three years). Consistency is the key, in my opinion, to maintaining your willingness to stick by an investment rule over the long haul, since no investment discipline beats the market every year.

USING EXCHANGE-TRADED FUNDS

An investor can employ The Seven Rules of Wall Street by investing either in sector-specific open-ended mutual funds or exchange-traded funds (ETFs). I prefer ETFs. Open-ended sector mutual funds are okay, but you never really know which stocks are owned by this active fund manager at any given point in time. With ETFs, however, you always know what is owned. A growing number of these baskets—or funds—replicate popular indexes, such as the Standard & Poor's 500 index and its sector indexes. Currently there are more than 800 ETFs. These "funds" are "traded" like stocks on "exchanges." That's why they are called exchange-traded funds. ETFs are commonly found on the New York Stock Exchange (NYSE), American Stock Exchange (ASE), and Nasdaq.

I also like ETFs because they are inexpensive. Just as with open-ended index mutual funds, the annual expense ratios for ETFs are typically very low. But unlike some open-ended mutual funds, ETFs have no front-end loads, or expenses for purchasing the fund. In addition, ETFs aren't saddled by 12b–1 fees, which is a cost paid to the fund family to continue marketing the fund to others. Other than expense ratio, the only cost for most ETFs is to trade on an exchange, which is very low today because of discount brokers.

There have been many articles written recently about how some ETFs have become overly esoteric by investing in a very small universe of stocks. I agree that investors may not get the returns they were hoping for from these thinly traded and narrowly focused ETFs. But you shouldn't experience that kind of illiquidity with the sector ETFs I reference in this book.

ETFs are equally weighted, fundamentally weighted, market-capitalization-weighted, or price-weighted. Please see the glossary for a thorough explanation of each method.

IMITATION CHALLENGES

Even though there are more than 800 ETFs, there are a limited number of them that mimic the composition of the 130 industries found in the S&P 500. Therefore, when developing industry-level portfolios, you typically have to select a stock to serve as a proxy, or representative, for that industry. I accomplish this by leveraging S&P equity analysts' expertise by selecting a stock within each industry that has the highest "buy, sell, or hold" ranking based on S&P's STARS (Stock Appreciation Ranking System). If more than one industry component has a similar high STARS, I choose the stock with the largest market value.

Sectors do not have a similar limitation, as there are nine sector-level ETFs representing the 10 sectors in the S&P 500. Since the Telecommunications Services sector has such few members, and represents only 3% of the total market value of the S&P 500, it is combined with the Information Technology sector in the market-cap-weighted ETFs, and is combined with the Utilities sector in the equally weighted ETFs.

Now it's time to get introduced to the Seven Rules of Wall Street.

THE SEVEN RULES THAT BEAT THE STREET

- **Rule 1—Let Your Winners Ride, but Cut Your Losers Short**
  Contrary to popular opinion, it's been more rewarding to invest in those industries that recorded the best price performances over the past year, while avoiding those with the worst. In this case, "Buy Low, Sell High" doesn't typically work in the short run!

- **Rule 2—As Goes January, So Goes the Year**
  The first month of the year has been very accurate in forecasting the coming year's price performance for equity markets, sectors, and industries. Find out how you can leverage this forecasting phenomenon.

- **Rule 3—Sell in May and Then Go Away**
  Want to make money when others don't? The market and most sectors typically take a "price-appreciation vacation" during the summer months. Find out which sectors have traditionally seen the summer months as their "days in the sun."

- **Rule 4—There's No Free Lunch on Wall Street (Oh Yeah, Who Says?)**
  When Tech goes up, what goes down? By diversifying among sectors that zig when others zag, some investors have historically been able to get both a higher return as well as lower risk. Why shouldn't you?

- **Rule 5—There's Always a Bull Market Someplace**
  Not all investors are like Fred Astaire on the dance floor. For some, it may be best to let the market take the lead. This rear-view mirror approach to investing has a time-tested track record for picking near-term winners. Ready to take a spin?

- **Rule 6—Don't Get Mad—Get Even!**
  From 2000 to 2002, the S&P 500 fell 49%. By 2005, it was still off by more than 25%. How could you have invested in the S&P 500, yet avoided such long-lasting portfolio carnage? Get small-cap performance with large-cap stability.
- **Rule 7—Don't Fight the Fed**
  The Federal Reserve controls the cost of cash. During periods of rising interest rates, there has traditionally been almost no place to hide. Yet when the Fed has begun cutting interest rates, the equity markets have usually soared. Will your portfolio be ready for the ride? Learn to identify which sectors are traditional leaders and laggards during these periods of interest-rate adjustments.

You got to know when to hold 'em, know when to fold 'em . . .

—KENNY ROGERS

RULE 1

LET YOUR WINNERS RIDE, BUT CUT YOUR LOSERS SHORT

WHICH PORTFOLIO WOULD YOU SELECT?

Suppose on New Year's Eve you asked a room full of investors to select a portfolio with the greatest chance of outperforming the S&P 500 in the coming calendar year. Which portfolio do you think they would choose? Would they select portfolio number 1, which consists of the 10 S&P 500 industries that posted the worst performances during the prior calendar year, or portfolio number 2, which contains the 10 industries with the best results from last year?

Some investors might loudly volunteer, "Buy the losers! You know, like the old adage, 'buy low, sell high.' I want *this* year's best performers, not *last* year's." On the other hand, there could be an equally fervent portion of the audience that shouts, "Stick with the winners! Momentum is on their side."

I have found that most people would have chosen portfolio number 1, the one with last year's dogs, concluding that the worst was over for these groups and only good times lay ahead. Well, do you know what? They would have been wrong! History tells us that portfolio number 2—last year's top performers—would have been the better choice.

BACKTESTING THE RULE

20

I started my backtest by developing two portfolios for 1970. I calculated the price performances for the 100 industries in the S&P 500 during 1969. I then sorted these industries high to low based on their price performance for that calendar year, and selected the 10 best and 10 worst industries.

During 1969, the best-performing industries were Alcoholic Beverages, Non-Alcoholic Beverages, Computer Hardware, Electrical Equipment, Health Care–Major Pharmaceuticals, Health Care–Medical Products & Supplies, Household Products, Lodging–Hotels, Personal Care, and Waste Management. These 10 industries became my "Winners" portfolio for 1970.

The worst-performing groups were Aerospace/Defense, Airlines, Chemicals, Entertainment, Footwear, Gold & Precious Metals Mining, Diversified Machinery, Oil–Domestic Integrated, Publishing, and Railroads. These 10 industries became my "Losers" portfolio for 1970. At the end of 1970, the price performances for these Winners and Losers portfolios were recorded.

At the start of each successive year, I performed the same process by populating the best and worst groups with a new set of 10 industries and computing their year-ahead performances. When I finished with 2007, I looked back and found some very enlightening results.

THE PROOF IS IN THE PUDDING

I found that the rule Let Your Winners Ride, but Cut Your Losers Short has been a time-tested adage for good reason. On average, the winners beat the market by a near two-to-one margin. The winners also beat the losers most years: seven out of every 10 years.

The losers, on the other hand, outperformed only marginally and suffered through a greater amount of annual price fluctuation. And they bested the "500" only 50% of the time. Figure 1.1 summarizes the returns for the S&P 500, the Losers and the Winners over the past 38 years for industries, and over 18 years for sectors.

FIGURE 1.1

They're Not Called Winners for Nothing

S&P 500 Sector & Industry Winners and Losers, 1970–2007					
Since 1970	**Average Annual Return**	**Compound Growth Rate**	**Standard Deviation**	**Risk-Adjusted Return**	**Frequency of Beating S&P 500**
S&P 500	8.8%	7.6%	16.1	0.55	NA
10 Industry Losers	10.8%	7.8%	25.4	0.42	50%
10 Industry Winners	16.1%	13.7%	23.3	0.69	71%
Since 1990					
S&P 500	10.4%	9.2%	16.5	0.63	NA
3 Sector Losers	10.2%	8.7%	17.5	0.58	41%
3 Sector Winners	12.7%	10.8%	20.6	0.62	71%

Source: Standard & Poor's Equity Research
Past performance is no guarantee of future results.

Allow me to go into a little more statistical detail now, and I promise to spare you in the future. Actually, I love going into detail. Whenever I do, however, I'm reminded of a conversation between my brother, his daughter, and myself as we were driving down the New Jersey Turnpike. My niece looked out the window and asked, "What's that building?" My brother answered, "That's a factory, dear." My niece said, "Oh," and that was it. Ten seconds later I said, "How come you didn't ask me?" She replied, "I didn't want to know that much about it."

UNDERSTANDING THE RESULTS

Take a look at Figure 1.1 and read from left to right. We see that since 1970 the S&P 500 posted an average annual gain in price of 8.8%. The "500" also posted a 7.6% compound annual growth rate. I believe it is important to show both measures of return.

Compound growth rates are the return a portfolio would experience over a particular time period by including the effects of compounding both increases and decreases. They are usually lower than average price changes and are more reflective of actual portfolio results. If your portfolio declined 50% in one year, but then rose 50% in the following year, the average annual percent change would be 0%. However, in real life, if your portfolio suffered through a 50% decline in one year, you would need a 100% advance in the following year just to break even! Compound growth rates show you what your portfolio would have experienced in real life.

The "500" also experienced a standard deviation of 16.1. Investors look to standard deviation as a measure of long-term annual performance fluctuation, or volatility. The S&P 500's standard deviation of 16.1 means that in two out of every three years the index posted an 8.8% return, give or take 16.1%.

In other words, over this 38-year period, two-thirds of all annual returns for the market were between +24.9% and −7.3%. I arrive at these numbers by adding and subtracting the 16.1% standard deviation from the 8.8% average annual return. So, 8.8% plus 16.1% equals 24.9%, whereas 8.8% minus 16.1% equals −7.3%. One encouraging statistic about the market's volatility is that the S&P 500 posted calendar-year declines in excess of 10% only six times— 1974 was the worst, falling 29.7%. Other double-digit decline years were 1973, 1977, 2000, 2001, and 2002. Year to date through November 28, 2008, the S&P 500 fell 39%, and is sure to prove a big calendar-year loser as well. Meanwhile, the S&P 500 recorded full-year advances of 10% or more 20 times; four calendar-year results exceeded 30%, with 1995 at the top of the heap, with a 34.1% surge.

The S&P 500's risk-adjusted return is calculated by dividing the return by the risk, or 8.8% divided by 16.1%. During this period it was 0.55. By itself, this number doesn't mean much. It is very useful, however, when deciding if the return offered by a more volatile technique has been worth the risk. A higher number is better than a lower one.

WINNERS AND LOSERS FOR A REASON

Figure 1.1 also shows that an investor who chose the Losers portfolio received a 10.8% annual return. This return was

200 basis points, or 2 percentage points, above the S&P 500's 8.8% return. Not bad. However, the Losers more-important 7.8% compound growth rate was only a shade above the market's 7.6% compound growth rate. In addition, the Losers portfolio experienced a surge in volatility, with a standard deviation of 25.4.

As a result, this portfolio posted a risk-adjusted return that was dramatically lower than that for the S&P 500 at 0.42. What's more, this portfolio beat the market only 50% of the time, as shown in the "Frequency of Beating the S&P 500" column. That was no better than a coin toss! As a result, I believe this portfolio's modest additional return was not worth the substantial increase in risk.

The investor who selected the Winners portfolio, however, received a 16.1% annual return. That's nearly a doubling of the market's return each year! It also posted a 13.7% compound growth rate—more than 600 basis points, or 6 percentage points, of annual outperformance.

Despite the jump in volatility to 23.3, I believe the return was worth the risk, since the risk-adjusted return was higher than the S&P 500's at 0.69. Finally, this portfolio beat the market more than seven times out of every 10. That's a 71% frequency of beating the S&P 500. How many Hall of Fame baseball players have a 710 batting average?

REASONS TO LOOK AT BOTH FORMS OF OUTPERFORMANCE

These portfolios are perfect examples of why I like to look at both average and compound annual returns. If a portfolio's return soared during a few years but was mediocre the rest of the time, the average returns may be misleading. These infrequent surges would skew the average return. They would make the investor believe the outperformance was consistent.

To overcome the effect of skewing, I think it is important to look at the frequencies of outperformance. I am like Pavlov's dog. I want to get fed on a fairly regular basis. Therefore, I need to see that an investment discipline, or rule, works more times than not. I prefer techniques that beat the market at least 67% (two-thirds) of the time.

SECTORS MAKE THE SCENE

Due to the recent introduction of exchange-traded funds (ETFs), I recently expanded this technique to include sectors within the S&P 500. There are 10 sectors within the S&P 500: Consumer Discretionary, Consumer Staples, Energy, Financials, Health Care, Industrials, Information Technology, Materials, Telecommunications Services, and Utilities. The 130 industries in the S&P 500 are assigned to one of these 10 sectors.

Consumer Discretionary companies offer products or services to a consumer that may be delayed if economic times are tough. They include industries such as autos, homebuilding, and retail. Consumer Staples, however, are goods and services that are needed when times are good or bad. They include food, beverage, and tobacco. Industrials are machinery, manufacturing, and transportation companies. The Materials sector, also called Basic Materials, includes chemicals, metals, and paper and forest products companies. Finally the Telecommunications Services sector consists of the wireless and wireline service providers. They provide the service. They don't manufacture the hardware, such as cell phone handsets. The communications equipment manufacturers are found in the Information Technology sector, along with other hardware and software providers.

27

The Sector Winners portfolio consisted of the three sectors with the highest prior-year performances. The Sector Losers portfolio was made up of the three sectors with the lowest returns in the prior year. As Figure 1.1 reveals, since 1990 the S&P 500 gained an average 10.4% per year, and recorded a compound growth rate of 9.2%. The "500" also posted a standard deviation of 16.5, and a risk-adjusted return of 0.63.

The Sector Losers portfolio gained an average 10.2% per year. That's only 20 basis points of underperformance. Its compound growth rate was 8.7%. This margin of under-performance was pretty thin, too. The Sector Losers port-folio also registered a standard deviation of 17.5. That translated to a below-market risk-adjusted return of 0.58. Lastly, it delivered a patience-trying 41% frequency of beating the S&P 500. In other words, it failed to beat the market in nearly six out of every 10 times.

The Sector Winners portfolio, on the other hand, gained an average 12.7% per year. That is 230 basis points of market outperformance. Its 10.8% compound growth rate also provided a more comforting margin of outperformance. The Sector Winners portfolio also saw a jump in standard deviation to 20.6. However, it still provided a market-equaling risk-adjusted return of 0.62. Lastly, it posted a 71% frequency of beating the S&P 500.

As a result of this favorable backtest, it appears to me that the Wall Street rule Let Your Winners Ride, but Cut Your Losers Short works well on both a sector and industry level.

BEHAVIOR MAY MAINTAIN SUCCESS

We have all heard many times over that past performance is no guarantee of future results. So why might this rule continue to provide market-beating performances on average in the years ahead? In a word: behavior.

How many investors do you know who own a stock that has recently hit a 52-week low are disappointed? Probably most. As a result, should this stock's share price begin to recover and approach breakeven, these investors are likely to "dump these dogs" and redirect their funds to more potentially rewarding opportunities.

Technicians refer to an abundance of investors in this position as "overhead resistance." As a result, it typically takes several tries over a number of years to break meaningfully above levels of significant overhead resistance. In other words, recoveries won't usually occur in a single year.

Conversely, how many investors are thrilled that their stocks have outpaced the overall market over the past year or maybe longer? And how many of these happy investors are dying to brag to others of their success? Finally, how many of the friends are likely to buy these outperformers, thus possibly extending this stock's winning streak? Probably a lot. And that could be why this rule may continue to outperform the overall market in the years to come, even though there's no guarantee that it will.

HISTORY IS A GREAT GUIDE, BUT IT'S NEVER GOSPEL

Always remember that history is a great guide, but it is never gospel. No investment technique works all of the time. The Let Your Winners Ride, but Cut Your Losers Short rule underperformed the broader market three years in a row, from 1987 to 1989, yet it beat the market 10 years straight from 1971 to 1980, including the mega-meltdown years of 1973 and 1974.

I find that investors typically fail before rules do. In other words, investors tend to give up on a rule after one or two years of underperformance—just when the rule is likely to work again. And to compound matters, they switch into another rule that just had a lengthy hot streak. As luck would have it, that rule would then likely hit a cold streak. In the end, an investor who doesn't stick with a particular discipline, and frequently changes allegiances, will likely give up on following rules altogether. So my recommendation is to either embrace a single rule that you favor most and stick with it, or embrace two rules, directing half of your money toward one rule and the other half toward the second rule.

BUILDING YOUR OWN WINNERS PORTFOLIO

How can you put together your own sector and industry Winners portfolios? Easy. At the beginning of each year, go to www.sandp.com to retrieve the S&P 500 Sector Scorecard for the year just ended. This is a free site. There is no charge for this data. The Web address is: http://www2.stan dardandpoors.com/portal/site/sp/en/us/page.topic/indices_ 500/2,3,2,2,0,0,0,0,0,5,10,0,0,0,0,0.html.

If that address changes in the future, just search on "Sector Scorecard" and you'll find it. I typically prepare this scorecard on New Year's Eve, and it is usually posted by noon on January 2. The scorecard shows the 10 sectors in alphabetical order, along with the industries within each sector, which are also shown in alphabetical order. The year-to-date (YTD) column will show the full-year returns for both the sectors and the industries.

ASSEMBLING YOUR WINNERS PORTFOLIOS

Let's assume you have $30,000 that you plan to use in order to put together a Sector Winners portfolio. One-third would be invested in each of the three sectors that posted the best performances in the prior calendar year.

As you may recall, there are 10 sectors in the S&P 500. They are Consumer Discretionary, Consumer Staples, Energy, Financials, Health Care, Industrials, Information Technology, Materials, Telecommunications Services, and Utilities. These 10 sectors contain the nearly 130 industries and 500 companies that make up the S&P 500.

The 2008 Winners portfolio consisted of the S&P 500 Energy, Materials, and Utilities sectors. They posted the best price performances of all 10 sectors during 2007. To invest in these sectors, you need to purchase equity instruments—sector exchange-traded funds, or ETFs—that mimic the makeup and performance of the S&P 500 sectors. One company has done this for us by creating ETFs that replicate S&P 500 sectors. These ETFs are called "Select Sector SPDRs." SPDR stands for S&P Depositary Receipts. These ETFs allow you to own a specific sector within the S&P 500. Visit www.sectorspdr.com to learn more about these sector ETFs.

You can buy and sell sector ETFs in the same way you buy stocks, through a broker or online.

If, on January 2, 2008, you chose to invest in the Select Sector SPDRs ETFs that mimic these S&P 500 sectors, you would have purchased an equal dollar amount of the Energy Select Sector ETF (XLE), the Materials Select Sector ETF (XLB), and the Utilities Select Sector ETF (XLU). You would then leave this portfolio untouched until January 2, 2009, when you would sell its contents and use the proceeds to invest in the 2009 Sector Winners portfolio.

Figure 1.2 gives a practical example of creating your own sector and industry Winners portfolios. To learn more about these and other sector ETFs, go to www.amex.com, the American Stock Exchange's Web site.

FIGURE 1.2

Creating Your Own Winners Portfolio for Sectors and Industries 2008

Evenly Dividing a Hypothetical $30,000 Among Portfolio Members					
Sector Winners Portfolio	**Select SPDR ETF Name**	**Ticker**	**12/31/07 Price**	**S&P STARS**	**No. of Shares**
Energy	Energy Sector SPDR	XLE	$79	NA	126
Materials	Materials Sector SPDR	XLB	$42	NA	241
Utilities	Utilities Sector SPDR	XLU	$42	NA	238
Industry Winners Portfolio	**Index Representative**	**Ticker**	**12/31/07 Price**	**S&P STARS**	**No. of Shares**
Agricultural Products	Archer-Daniels-Midland	ADM	$46	4	65
Coal & Consumable Fuels	Peabody Energy	BTU	$62	4	48
Construction & Engineering	Flour Corp.	FLR	$146	4	21
Diversified Metals & Mining	Freeport-MacMoRan	FCX	$102	3	29
Education Services	Apollo Group	APOL	$70	4	43
Fertilizers & Agricultural Chemicals	Monsanto	MON	$112	3	27
Health Care Services	Lab. Corp. of America	LH	$76	5	39
Industrial Gases	Air Products & Chemicals	APD	$99	3	30
Internet Retail	IAC/InterActive Corp.	IACI	$27	4	111
Oil & Gas Equipment & Services	Baker Hughes, Inc.	BHI	$81	5	37

33

Source: Standard & Poor's Equity Research

SECTORS ARE EASIER THAN INDUSTRIES

Creating your own Industry Winners portfolio is a bit trickier than developing a sector portfolio. Why? That's because there are very few ETFs that mimic industries within the S&P 500. I solved this by selecting a single stock to serve as an industry representative or proxy. What's more, I leveraged S&P equity analysts' expertise by selecting the stock that had the highest investment ranking as of December 31, 2007.

You can do the same thing by signing on to www.spout look.com and performing a stock screen, searching for the companies within each industry that have the highest S&P STARS (buy, sell, or hold ranking). If you choose not to subscribe to this service at $20 per month, I suggest taking advantage of your local library. Typically a larger county or business school library will subscribe to S&P's NetAdvantage product. Again, sign on, and perform a search looking for the highest-ranked stocks within each of the 10 industries that had the highest prior-year returns. If you find that there is more than one stock with the highest investment ranking, select the issue with the largest market value. Market value, sometimes called "market cap," is computed by multiplying the number of common shares outstanding by the share price.

All industries should have one representative company. You'll notice that some issues have 3-STARS, or "hold" rankings by S&P analysts. That's okay, provided they are the companies with the highest STARS rankings in that industry.

Figure 1.2 also shows how you would have distributed your hypothetical $30,000 to develop an Industry Winners portfolio. Each stock in this portfolio would represent one-tenth of the value of the total portfolio, or about $3,000 each. Just as with the Sector Winners portfolio, you would leave this portfolio untouched until January 2, 2009, when you would sell its contents and use the proceeds to invest in the 2009 Industry Winners portfolio.

You now have all the information you need to develop your own Winners portfolios. Good luck.

Investors are like dieters. They look upon January as a new beginning.

—SAM STOVALL

AS GOES JANUARY, SO GOES THE YEAR

After presenting the Let Your Winners Ride portfolio concept to a group of investors, I almost always get one individual who sheepishly approaches me and asks in hushed tones—as he looks around the room in a suspicious manner as if he were about to reveal state secrets—"It's nice to know that *last* year's outperformers will also deliver market-beating returns this year, but can't you tell me which sectors and industries are going to be *this* year's best performers?" To their surprise, my answer is, "Yes. I know of a technique that will help spot the better performers in the coming year. It's called the 'January Barometer portfolios of sectors and industries,' which are derived from the old Wall Street saying 'As Goes January, So Goes the Year.'"

This adage was discovered and popularized by my friend Yale Hirsch, publisher of the *Stock Trader's Almanac*. His son Jeff continues to monitor this and other interesting investment tidbits.[1]

JANUARY: A DIVINING ROD FOR THE S&P 500

So, now is the moment of truth. How do I profess to know how to spot those sectors and industries within the S&P 500 that likely will become the best performers for the coming year? I accomplish this by monitoring the S&P 500 in the first month of each year.

As seen in Figure 2.1, the S&P 500's performance in January has become a very good gauge of its performance during the remainder of the year. Since 1945, the S&P 500 rose 41 times in the month of January. It fell 22 times. Whenever the S&P 500 advanced in price in January, the S&P 500 continued to rise an average 11.6% during the remaining 11 months of the year. That's substantially higher than the average 7.3% price gain for the S&P 500 during all 11-month periods since World War II. Finally, this early upward "directional signal" was correct 85% of the time.

---

[1] Visit www.stocktradersalmanac.com to learn more about their monthly and annual publications.

FIGURE 2.1

A Divining Rod for the Rest of the Year

When the S&P 500's January % Change Was	No. of Times It Occurred	S&P 500 Change in Rest of Year	Indicator Was Correct
January Barometer, 1945–2007			
Up	41	11.6%	85%
Down	22	−0.7%	45%
All Years	63	7.3%	NA

Source: Standard & Poor's Equity Research
Past performance is no guarantee of future results.

I have found no other month that works so well as a year-ahead indicator.

Whenever the S&P 500 declined in January, this benchmark went on to decline an average 0.7% in the remaining 11 months of the year. This performance obviously doesn't mean you would have made a lot of money shorting the market. In fact, since the indicator was correct only 45% of the time, this early downward "directional signal" was a better indicator of cautiousness than of outright bearishness. Its two biggest misses occurred in 1982 and 2003 when it signaled a down year but the S&P 500 rose 16.8% and 29.9%, respectively, in the remaining 11 months of the year. On the other hand, it did an excellent job warning investors of tough times ahead in 1973, 1974, 2000, and

2002, when the S&P 500 subsequently fell 15.9%, 29.0%, 5.3%, and 22.2%, respectively. It was also negative in 2008.

HIGH LEVEL OF ACCURACY EXPECTED

Even though past performance is no guarantee of future results, I think this old saying will continue to offer sound predictions in the years ahead, since it mirrors investor behavior. I believe investors are a lot like dieters; they look to January as a new beginning. At the start of the year, investors frequently have a lot of cash on the sidelines. This is usually because they may have sold losing securities late in the prior year to offset the tax consequences of profits taken from winning investments. As a result, this money will likely be reinvested in January. What's more, these investors will likely stick with these new commitments for at least 12 months in order to take advantage of the more favorable tax treatment offered by long-term capital gains.

JANUARY ALSO SPOTS INDUSTRY AND SECTOR STANDOUTS

Due to the success of the January Barometer in forecasting the direction of the S&P 500 during the remainder of the year, Yale Hirsch, from the *Stock Trader's Almanac*, and I wondered whether January could also be a good predictor of year-ahead performances for sectors and industries in the S&P 500. The answer is a resounding "yes." As a result of this success, the January Barometer portfolio is highlighted each year in Yale's *Stock Trader's Almanac*.

POWERFUL PERFORMANCES

Developing a January Barometer portfolio for either sectors or industries is amazingly simple—just select the three S&P 500 sectors, or 10 industries, that posted the best performances during January and hold them for a year. That's all you have to do.

You may be surprised to discover the magnitude and frequency of rewards you could have reaped by taking a cue from a single month's performance (see Figure 2.2). You may also be surprised to find out that the January Barometer portfolios frequently beat the market whether the S&P 500 rose or fell in January. You even find out which sectors or industries to avoid. Just as with the Let Your Winners Ride portfolio, the performances of the industries and sectors in the January Barometer portfolio show that investors can save themselves a lot of heartache by avoiding the three sectors and 10 industries that posted the weakest performances during this opening month of the year.

FIGURE 2.2

Know What the Sectors and Industries Will Do Ahead of Time

January Barometer Portfolios, 1/30/70–1/30/08					
12-Month Returns Since 1970	Average Annual Return	Compound Growth Rate	Standard Deviation	Risk- Adjusted Return	Frequency of Beating S&P 500
S&P 500	8.7%	7.6%	15.0	0.51	NA
Best 10 Industries in January	18.2%	15.9%	24.3	0.65	71%
Worst 10 Industries in January	5.6%	6.2%	18.2	0.34	39%
12-Month Returns Since 1990					
S&P 500	9.5%	8.3%	16.3	0.58	NA
Best 3 Sectors in January	14.2%	12.4%	20.5	0.69	75%
Worst 3 Sectors in January	6.6%	5.6%	14.6	0.45	40%

Source: Standard & Poor's Equity Research
Past performance is no guarantee of future results.

STICK WITH INDUSTRY LEADERS

To backtest this investment discipline, I again computed performances for the industries in the S&P 500 from 1970 and for sectors in the S&P 500 from 1990. The results were eye-opening.

Reading Figure 2.1 from left to right, we see that since 1970 the S&P 500 posted a 12-month (January 30 to January 30) average price change of 8.7%. Its compound annual growth rate was 7.6%. Remember that the average annual percent change is the simple arithmetic mean of price changes over a specified period of time. It is usually higher than the compound annual growth rate. The S&P 500's standard deviation—the measure of annual price swings—was 15.0. Its risk-adjusted return was therefore 0.51. Finally, the S&P 500 obviously doesn't have a frequency of beating itself.

The 10 industries in the S&P 500 that recorded the highest price performances in the month of January alone went on to record an average 18.2% price appreciation in the following 12 months. That's an average annual outperformance of the S&P 500 by 950 basis points, or nearly 10 percentage points, per year! On a compound annual basis, the 15.9% average compound rate of growth for the January Barometer portfolio for industries swamped the S&P 500's compound growth rate of 7.6% by a more than 2-to-1 margin!

Of course, into everyone's life a little rain must fall, so it should come as no surprise that the January Barometer portfolio for industries recorded a higher standard deviation than did the S&P 500 at 24.3. Because the January Barometer's risk-adjusted return of 0.65 was higher than the market's 0.51, however, I believe the substantial additional return was well worth the increased risk. Finally, the frequency of beating the S&P 500 for the January Barometer portfolio for industries was very reassuring at 71%.

AVOID INDUSTRY LAGGARDS

The 10 industries that recorded the lowest price performances in January continued their laggard ways, by registering an average annual gain of 5.6%. This was more than 300 basis points below the S&P 500's average annual return. Not surprisingly, these industries that posted the lowest returns in January also recorded the weakest compound growth rates in the following 12 months. These industries underperformed the S&P 500 by 1.4% each year.

To add insult to injury, not only did the 10 January also-rans underperform in the year ahead, but they also posted an increase in volatility. Their standard deviation of 18.2 was higher than the S&P 500's. As a result, the 10 industries that recorded the weakest results in January also recorded an unappetizingly low risk-adjusted return in the coming 12-month period on average.

Finally, we see that since 1970 the 10 worst-performing industries in January posted an average annual return that beat the S&P 500 only 39% of the time. Need I say more as to why one should typically avoid the January laggards?

SECTOR LEADERS

Sector performance results—for both the best and worst performers in January—were consistent with the results for the best- and worst-performing industries.

As Figure 2.2 reveals, the three sector indexes in the S&P 500 that posted the best performances during January went on to record an average annual price increase of 14.2% in the following 12-month period. This was nearly 500 basis points better than the market's average annual advance. In addition, the three best sectors posted a 12.4% compound annual growth rate. This resulted in an average market outperformance of more than 4 percentage points per year.

Even though 4 percentage points of outperformance per year may sound trivial, just consider that $1,000 invested in the January Barometer portfolio for sectors in 1990 was worth $8,167 through January 2008, versus $4,189 for $1,000 invested in the S&P 500 Index (excluding dividends).

The standard deviation of the top three sectors' average annual performance was 20.5. This was higher than the market's 16.3. I believe that the superior return for January's three best-performing sectors was worth the increased volatility, as the sectors' risk-adjusted return of 0.69 was higher than the S&P 500's 0.58.

The frequency with which the January Barometer portfolio for sectors beat the S&P 500 is possibly the best of all statistics on this table. Imagine finding an investment discipline that has beaten the market three out of every four times! Not only would you have gotten the satisfaction of seeing your portfolio grow over time, but I think the consistency with which it outperformed the market would have made for many restful nights.

SECTOR LAGGARDS

By now you probably won't be surprised when I tell you that the three weakest-performing sectors in January subsequently recorded subpar performances in the following 12 months, compared with the S&P 500. You might, however, be surprised by the magnitude of that underperformance.

The three sectors that posted the worst performances in January recorded average annual returns that underperformed the S&P 500 by nearly 300 basis points per year in each of the following 18 years. Their compound rates of growth weren't much better. They lagged the market by 270 basis points, or 2.7 percentage points, per year. And even though the standard deviation of the three worst performers was surprisingly low at 14.6, the lower volatility didn't help the risk-adjusted return enough to make it a worthwhile alternative. It still came out below the market's, indicating to me that even this reduced volatility did not make up for the poor average performances.

The nail in the three worst sectors' coffin, in my opinion, was the 40% frequency of beating the S&P 500. More than any other statistic, I think this one would turn off investors who might have selected the three worst-performing sectors as an investment discipline.

KEY TAKEAWAYS

As I have shown you, the S&P 500's performance in January has been a reliable barometer for the market's performance during the remainder of the year. In addition, sector and industry performances in January have been helpful indicators of future areas of market outperformance. For those investors who choose to follow the As Goes January rule, I advise sticking with the winning sectors and industries from January—while avoiding the losers—if you want to be holding the likely outperformers 12 months later.

What's more, be aware that, since 1945, February has been the second-worst month for the S&P 500. The broad market declined an average 0.3% in February versus an average advance of 0.7% for the S&P 500 during all 12 months. In addition, the S&P 500 fell in February 50% of the time versus the average 41% frequency of decline for the S&P 500 during all 12 months. I point this out so you don't become instantly disappointed with the January Barometer portfolio as a result of typical seasonal market actions.

You're probably dying to find out in which month the S&P 500 has posted its worst results. The answer is September. The S&P 500 fell an average 0.63% in September since the end of World War II. Also, the market declined 56% of the time. In fact, whether you look back to 1990, 1970, 1945, or 1929, the average return for the S&P 500 has been negative in September.

As with all historical performances, remember that what worked in the past may not always work in the future. For example, the January Barometer portfolio for industries underperformed the broader market four years in a row from 1994 to 1997. This portfolio saw gains in three of these four years but recorded gains that were below the market's. Yet it outperformed the S&P 500 eight years straight from 1998 to 2005. Therefore, an investor who selects this technique to follow should be aware that, like a home-run-hitting baseball player, this portfolio might undergo a hitting slump every now and again.

BUILDING YOUR OWN JANUARY BAROMETER PORTFOLIOS

You can put together your own sector and industry January Barometer portfolios as easily as assembling your Winners portfolios from Rule 1. On the first trading day of February, go to www.sandp.com to retrieve the January month-end S&P 500 Sector Scorecard. This is a free site. There is no charge to retrieve this data. Remember, if this address changes in the future, just search on "Sector Scorecard" and you'll find it.

ASSEMBLY EXAMPLE

Let's assume you have $30,000 that you plan to use to put together a January Barometer portfolio for sectors. You would invest one-third in each of the three sectors that posted the best one-month performances during January.

As you may recall, there are 10 sectors in the S&P 500. They are Consumer Discretionary, Consumer Staples, Energy, Financials, Health Care, Industrials, Information Technology, Materials, Telecommunications Services, and Utilities. These 10 sectors contain the nearly 130 industries and 500 companies that make up the S&P 500.

The 2008–2009 January Barometer portfolio for sectors consisted of the S&P 500 Consumer Discretionary, Financials, and Materials sectors. They posted the best price performances of all 10 sectors during January 2008. To invest in these sectors, you need to purchase equity instruments—sector exchange-traded funds (ETFs)—that mimic the makeup and performance of the S&P 500 sectors. The Select Sector SPDRs do this. You can buy and sell sector ETFs in the same way you buy stocks, through a broker or online.

49

On February 1, 2008, purchase an equal dollar amount of the Consumer Discretionary Select Sector ETF (XLY), the Financials Select Sector ETF (XLF), and the Materials Select Sector ETF (XLB). Then leave this portfolio untouched until February 1, 2009. At that time, you would sell your holdings in XLY, XLF, and XLB. Use the proceeds to invest in the 2009–2010 January Barometer portfolio for sectors. This new portfolio will consist of the three S&P 500 sectors that posted the highest returns during January 2009.

FIGURE 2.3

Creating Your Own January Barometer Portfolios for Sectors and Industries 2008–2009

Evenly Dividing a Hypothetical $30,000 Among Portfolio Members					
January Barometer Portfolio for Sectors	**ETF Name**	**Ticker**	**2/1/2008 Price**	**S&P STARS**	**No. of Shares**
Consumer Discretionary	Consumer Discretionary SPDR	XLY	$33	NA	303
Financials	Financials SPDR	XLF	$30	NA	333
Materials	Materials SPDR	XLB	$41	NA	244
Industries	**Index Representative**				
Education Services	Apollo Group 'A'	APOL	$81	4	37
General Merchandise Stores	Big Lots	BIG	$18	4	167
Gold	Newmont Mining	NEM	$53	3	56
Home Furnishings	Leggett & Platt	LEG	$19	3	158
Home Improvement Retail	Home Depot	HD	$30	4	100
Homebuilding	D.R. Horton, Inc.	DHI	$17	4	177
Homefurnishing Retail	Bed, Bath and Beyond	BBBY	$32	4	94
Leisure Products	Mattel, Inc.	MAT	$21	5	143
Regional Banks	PNC Financial Services	PNC	$66	3	45
Trucking	Ryder System	R	$55	4	54

Source: Standard & Poor's Equity Research

Figure 2.3 gives a practical example of creating your own January Barometer portfolios for sectors and industries.

SECTORS ARE EASIER THAN INDUSTRIES

Remember that creating your own January Barometer portfolio for industries will be a bit trickier than developing a sector portfolio. That's because there are very few ETFs that mimic industries within the S&P 500. I solved this by selecting a single stock to serve as an industry representative or proxy. What's more, I leveraged S&P equity analysts' expertise by selecting the stock that had the highest investment ranking as of January 31, 2008.

You can do the same thing by signing on to www.spout look.com and performing a stock screen, searching for the companies within each industry that have the highest S&P STARS (buy, sell, or hold ranking). If you choose not to subscribe to this service at $20 per month, I suggest taking advantage of your local library. Typically a larger county or business school library will subscribe to S&P's NetAdvantage product. Again, sign on, and perform a search looking for the highest-ranked stocks within each of the 10 industries that had the highest returns in January. If you find that there is more than one stock with the highest investment ranking, select the issue with the largest market value. Market value, sometimes called "market cap," is computed by multiplying the number of common shares outstanding by the share price.

All industries should have one representative company. You'll notice that some issues in my hypothetical portfolios have 3-STARS, or "hold" rankings by S&P analysts. That's okay, provided they were the companies with the highest STARS rankings in that industry.

Figure 2.3 also shows how you would have distributed your hypothetical $30,000 to develop a January Barometer portfolio for industries. Just as with the sector portfolio, you would leave this portfolio untouched until February 1, 2009, when you would sell its contents and use the proceeds to invest in the January Barometer portfolio for industries for 2009–2010.

You have now developed your own January Barometer portfolios. Good job. Now take the rest of the year off.

During the summer, investors focus more on their tans than their portfolios.

—Sam Stovall

SELL IN MAY AND THEN GO AWAY

Sell in May and then go away. This adage has been around for decades and maybe even centuries. Do a search on the Web and you will likely find reference to an Old English saying: "Sell in May and then go away. Do not return until St. Leger's Day."

This saying has favorable investment implications. No matter whether you look back to 1990, 1970, 1945, or 1929, you'll find that the same thing has been true: the S&P 500's average price change has been substantially higher during the six months from November 1 through April 30 than it has been during the six months from May 1 through October 31. What's more, this rule has been successful two out of every three years. These odds are good enough, in my opinion, to keep me wanting to go away in May. But should you sell out of stocks and hide out in cash during

FIGURE 3.1

Equal Periods, Unequal Performances

	S&P 500 Price Return Data Through 10/31/08		
	S&P 500 Price Change		Nov.–Apr. Beat May–Oct.
Since	Nov.–Apr.	May–Oct.	
1929	4.9%	1.6%	68%
1945	6.8%	1.1%	72%
1970	6.6%	0.6%	72%
1990	6.2%	0.5%	68%

Source: Standard & Poor's Equity Research
Past performance is no guarantee of future results.

the May–October period? I'll show you why that would not be such a good idea.

Take a look at Figure 3.1. Since 1945, the S&P 500 posted an average price gain of 6.8% during the November–April period, versus a rise of only 1.1% from May to October. In addition, the price performance of the S&P 500 from November to April beat the price change during the following May–October period 72% of the time. There may be several reasons for this pronounced seasonal strength and weakness.

REASONS FOR THE SEMIANNUAL SOFTNESS

Here are what I consider to be the three main reasons for seasonal weakness during the May–October period:

- Vacations
- Earnings reality overtaking optimism
- A lack of capital inflows

Let's look at each of these, in turn.

Vacations

From the perspective of seasonal sluggishness, history shows that the S&P 500 has posted its weakest three-month average performance in the third quarter, as investors may be focusing more on their tans than on their portfolios. In other words, investors' attention is more likely being paid to their vacation plans than to their investment strategies. And the data bears this out.

As shown in Figure 3.2, since 1945, the S&P 500 advanced only 0.3% in the third quarter of each year (July through September) versus 2.1% for the first quarter, 1.9% for the second, a whopping 4.0% for the fourth quarter, and an average 2.1% for all four quarters of the year. In addition, while the S&P 500 rose 65% of the time during all four quarters of the year, it advanced only 57% of the time in the third quarter.

Earnings

End-of-year earnings revisions may also be a reason the market performs poorly in the third quarter. After first-quarter

FIGURE 3.2

During the Summer, Investors Focus More on Their Tans Than on Their Portfolios

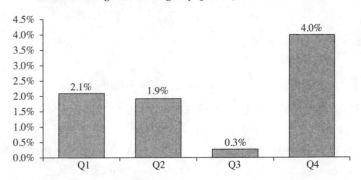

S&P 500 Average Price Changes by Quarter, 1945–October 2008

Source: Standard & Poor's Equity Research
Past performance is no guarantee of future results.

results have been released, and if they haven't been up to expectations, an investor might remark, "Oh heck, we've got three more quarters in which to make up the difference." If the second quarter is also a disappointment, they may start sounding like old diehard Brooklyn Dodgers fans: "Just wait'll the second half!" But should the third quarter look like it's going to miss expectations as well, investors usually don't wait around. Like a veteran retailer, they'll "mark 'em down, and move 'em out." As a result, this could be a reason the S&P 500 posted its worst average monthly performance in September, whether you look back to 1929, 1945, or 1970.

We can clearly see from Figure 3.3 that since 1945 the S&P 500 declined an average 0.8% in September. The S&P 500, on the other hand, posted an average advance of 0.6% for all 12 months of the year. In addition, while the S&P 500 declined only 41% of the time during all months, it declined 56% of the time in September.

October is historically a month in which the market establishes a bottom. Therefore, the S&P 500 enters November at a fairly low level compared to other months.

FIGURE 3.3

Forget the Ides of March, Watch Out for September

S&P 500 Price Changes and Frequencies of Declines Through 10/31/08											

S&P 500 Average Monthly Price Changes											
Since	Jan.	Feb.	Mar.	Apr.	May	Jun.	Jul.	Aug.	Sep.	Oct.	Nov.	Dec.
1929	1.4%	−0.1%	0.2%	1.2%	−0.1%	0.9%	1.4%	0.8%	−1.3%	0.2%	0.5%	1.4%
1945	1.3%	−0.3%	1.0%	1.4%	0.4%	0.1%	0.7%	0.0%	−0.8%	0.8%	1.3%	1.8%
1970	1.4%	0.1%	0.8%	1.1%	0.6%	0.3%	0.1%	0.3%	−1.0%	0.5%	1.4%	1.7%
1990	0.4%	−0.1%	0.7%	1.4%	1.7%	−0.5%	0.0%	−0.8%	−1.0%	1.1%	1.9%	1.8%

S&P 500 Average Frequencies of a Price Decline											
Since	Jan.	Feb.	Mar.	Apr.	May	Jun.	Jul.	Aug.	Sep.	Oct.	Nov.	Dec.
1929	35%	49%	40%	40%	44%	44%	45%	40%	56%	43%	42%	28%
1945	36%	50%	36%	33%	42%	48%	48%	44%	56%	39%	35%	24%
1970	38%	46%	36%	36%	41%	44%	59%	41%	56%	44%	32%	26%
1990	37%	42%	37%	32%	26%	47%	58%	42%	53%	32%	28%	22%

Source: Standard & Poor's Equity Research
Past performance is no guarantee of future results.

This gives the November–April period the advantage of starting at a lower base. In addition, November is also the time of year that analysts begin looking ahead by five quarters, rather than just focusing on the final one or two.

Lack of Capital

The above-average strength in the November–April period also may be aided by large cash infusions into the market during this stretch of time. Wall Street bonuses are typically paid by March of each year. They are therefore likely invested in the market soon thereafter. Next, should people be due a tax refund, they will likely file their returns early. This will allow them to invest their proceeds before the end of April. Third, IRAs for the prior tax year need to be funded by April 15 of each year. Most tax filers I know—especially if they have to pay anything—are procrastinators. Therefore, many IRA contributions are probably made just before the tax deadline. Finally 401(k) contribution limits are typically fulfilled early, mainly due to bonuses being paid so early in the year.

SHOULD YOU REALLY GO AWAY?

Since 1945, the S&P 500 posted a 6.8% average gain from November through April. It recorded only a 1.1% advance from May through October. I don't think anyone would question that one six-month period was better than the other. But would it have been wise to "go away" by selling out of stocks and hiding out in cash during the May–October period? Except for 2008, it usually has not been a good idea.

The average advance of 1.1% for the S&P 500 is still similar to what an investor would have received from a money market fund or savings account during the typical six-month period. Besides, investors have to consider transaction costs and tax consequences of selling out. Most important, they may miss out on an unexpected summertime surge in stock prices. These considerations might make me suggest that investors ignore this rule rather than embrace it. Unless, of course, an investor could identify a more attractive alternative to a money market in which to invest during this seasonally slow period. That's where sector funds and ETFs make this rule an attractive investment discipline.

ONLY IF YOU HEAD TOWARD THE RIGHT SECTORS

On the S&P 500 level, we are now aware that it isn't worth our time selling in May and waiting for October. But maybe this rule could be improved if we looked beneath the surface at sectors within the S&P 500. Do some sectors have their day in the summertime sun, while others skate along smoothly in winter? History says "yes," as seen below.

NOVEMBER TO APRIL: DOMINATED BY CYCLICAL SECTORS

Figure 3.4 shows us that in the past 18 years (which is as far back as S&P has sector data), the S&P 500 Financials, Industrials, and Materials sectors posted the highest average price appreciations. In addition, these sectors beat the S&P 500 67% of the time or better during this six-month period.

FIGURE 3.4

Investors Have Played It Safe in the Summer

	Nov.–April		May–Oct.	
	Frequencies of Beating the S&P 500 by Season, 4/30/90–10/31/08			
Sector	Average Price Change	Freq. of Beating S&P 500	Average Price Change	Freq. of Beating S&P 500
Consumer Discretionary	9.6%	50%	−2.0%	42%
Consumer Staples	4.7%	56%	4.3%	68%
Energy	8.6%	50%	1.4%	47%
Financials	8.9%	67%	0.6%	53%
Health Care	5.3%	44%	4.4%	63%
Industrials	9.1%	78%	−1.2%	21%
Information Technology	8.7%	56%	2.3%	58%
Materials	3.3%	72%	−3.5%	32%
Telecommunication Services	2.2%	33%	0.7%	58%
Utilities	3.4%	39%	1.1%	47%
S&P 500	**6.7%**	**NA**	**0.5%**	**NA**

Source: Standard & Poor's Equity Research Services
Past performance is no guarantee of future results.

The Consumer Discretionary sector actually had the second-highest average price advance at 9.6%, but since it beat the market only 50% of the time, I chose not to highlight it. Also, Energy and Information Technology warrant mentioning, since they each advanced an average of 8.6% or more during the November–April period. However, again I point out that their frequencies of beating the S&P 500 were no better than a coin toss.

CYCLICAL OVER DEFENSIVE

It should come as no surprise that when the cyclical sectors do well, the defensive ones don't. Who wants to play it safe when prices are jumping? Defensive stocks—such as food, beverage, and pharmaceutical issues—experience fairly static demand during good and bad times. As a result, they tend to be the also-rans when the market is hot. This is borne out by the subpar average performances, and frequencies of beating the market, by the S&P 500 Consumer Staples, Health Care, Utilities, and Telecommunications Services sectors in the November–April period.

STAPLES AND HEALTH CARE DO BEST IN THE MAY–OCTOBER PERIOD

During the May–October period, however, it's a different story. The year 2008 was no exception. While the overall market barely has been keeping its head above water, the defensive issues are frolicking in the surf. Figure 3.4 shows that the highest price advances came from the Consumer Staples and Health Care sectors. They also beat the S&P 500 more frequently than other sectors.

I can understand Consumer Staples and Health Care doing well during this period of weak overall market returns. I've always said, "When the going gets tough, the tough go eating, smoking, and drinking—and to the doctor if they overdo it!" It's not that people prefer to get hip replacements in the summer more than at any other time of the year. I believe Health Care and Consumer Staples do better during challenging times for the overall market because investors would rather embrace more defensive sectors than bail out of stocks all together.

Honorable mention should go to the Information Technology sector. Since 1990, it posted a 2.3% average price advance during the May–October period, which was twice the market's gain. Tech stocks also beat the S&P 500 58% of the time. However, I don't include this sector as a summertime standout. I believe the Information Technology sector showed better-than-average results due more to the tech bubble of the late 1990s than as a result of defensive characteristics. In the future, it may end up posting returns that are closer to other cyclical sectors the further we get from that abnormal half decade.

TURNING THIS KNOWLEDGE INTO A SUCCESSFUL STRATEGY

Taking this sector-strength discovery one step further, I wondered how someone's portfolio would have performed if they had split the year in two. How would their portfolio returns have looked if they had been invested in the S&P 500 from November to April but then invested in either of the two defensive sectors during this "go-away" period of May to October?

Figure 3.5 tells a fairly convincing story, in my view. Had an investor stuck with the S&P 500 during all 12 months of the year from April 30, 1990, through October 31, 2008, they would have experienced a compound annual return of 5.8% (not including dividends reinvested). However, had someone invested in the S&P 500 from November to April, and then switched into either the S&P Consumer Staples or Health Care sectors from May to October, that person would have recorded a compound return in excess of the S&P 500's by more than 400 basis points (4 percentage points) per year! What's more, this rotational strategy beat the market an average 61% of the time using the S&P 500 Health Care sector and 67% using the S&P 500 Consumer Staples sector. Again, this frequency of beating the market is enough to keep me interested in this investment rule.

FIGURE 3.5

Make Your Returns Sizzle in the Summer

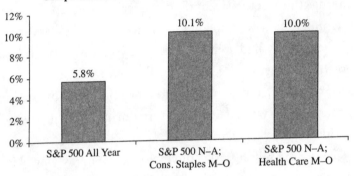

Compound Annual Growth Rates, April 1990-October 2008

Source: Standard & Poor's Equity Research
Past performace is no guarantee of future results.

66

SIMPLE SUCCESS

In summary, investors who were in the S&P 500 Index from November through April of each year and then in either Consumer Staples or Health Care during May through October, could have improved on the S&P 500's 5.8% compound growth rate by 4 percentage points per year. From April 30, 1990, through October 31, 2008, they could have turned a 5.8% return into a 10.0% annual compound rate of return. They could have turned their $1,000 initial investment into $2,929 by investing in the S&P 500 (excluding dividends). Or, by following this rule, could have grown it to $6,121. Sweet!

In 2008, while the S&P 500 fell by more than 30% from May through October, the S&P Consumer Staples and Health Care sectors fell by about half that amount, improving not only on their frequency of beating the S&P 500, but also the margin by which their average compound return beat the market.

Please allow me to take this opportunity to throw some cold water over you by reminding you that there is also no guarantee that what worked in the past will continue to work in the future.

BUILDING YOUR OWN "SELL IN MAY" PORTFOLIO

67

Assembling a Sell in May portfolio is even easier than putting together Winners or January Barometer portfolios, because it can be done entirely with ETFs.

Using Consumer Staples

Let's assume you have $30,000 that you plan to use to assemble a Sell in May portfolio. On the close of trading on April 30 (or the last trading day of the month), invest the entire $30,000 in the Consumer Staples Select Sector ETF (XLP). In 2008, XLP closed at $27.65 on April 30, which would have enabled you to purchase 1,084 shares.

Do nothing with this investment for six months.

Toward the close of trading on the last day of October, sell your 1,084 shares of XLP and invest all of the proceeds in the S&P 500 Depositary Receipts ETF (SPY). Leave this portfolio untouched for another six months, when you will sell your holdings in SPY and use the proceeds to invest in XLP once again.

This owning of SPY from November through April, followed by the owning of XLP from May through October, would occur in perpetuity.

Substituting Health Care

If you prefer to invest in the Health Care sector rather than the Consumer Staples sector, you simply substitute the Health Care Select Sector SPDR ETF (XLV) for the Consumer Staples Select Sector SPDR ETF (XLP) in the May–October period. In 2008, XLV closed at $35.72 on April 30, which would have enabled you to purchase 840 shares.

You would continue to own the SPY from November through April.

Diversifying with Consumer Staples and Health Care

You may prefer to hedge your bet by investing in both the Consumer Staples and Health Care sectors during the May–October period. In this case, toward the end of trading on the last day of April, invest half of your money in the Consumer Staples Select Sector ETF (XLP) and the other half in the Health Care Select Sector SPDR ETF (XLV). On April 30, 2008, you would have purchased 542 shares of XLP and 420 shares of XLV. It's as simple as that.

Figure 3.6 gives practical examples of creating the three versions of your own Sell in May portfolio.

Now sit back and let the market work its magic.

FIGURE 3.6

Creating Your Own Sell in May Portfolio

Buy and Sell at the End of the Last Trading Day of April and October											
Jan.	Feb.	Mar.	Apr.	May	Jun.	Jul.	Aug.	Sep.	Oct.	Nov.	Dec.

Option #1 -- Consumer Staples
Sell SPY / Buy XLP — Sell XLP / Buy SPY

Option #2 -- Health Care
Sell SPY / Buy XLV — Sell XLV / Buy SPY

Option #3 -- 1/2 Staples, 1/2 Health Care
Sell SPY / Buy XLP / Buy XLV — Sell XLP / Sell XLV / Buy SPY

Diversification is the only free lunch on Wall Street.

—A POPULAR INVESTMENT ADAGE

THERE'S NO FREE LUNCH ON WALL STREET (OH YEAH, WHO SAYS?)

If Sir Isaac Newton had a law of motion related to the stock market, it probably would have sounded like "for every level of return, there's an equivalent level of risk," meaning that the higher the returns you hope to achieve, the greater amount of risk you should be willing to accept.

It's just like what Mom always said: "If it sounds too good to be true, it probably is." And the same goes for stocks— generally. If you expect a high-price return, then you have to expect to experience an elevated level of risk, either in the form of price volatility or the potential loss of your original investment. And the logic for this is fairly straightforward. If you could get something for nothing, it wouldn't take long before many others joined you in this investment. And as more people would learn about it and buy into it, the potential to exploit any price inefficiency would evaporate. It's the simple principal of arbitrage.

Sometimes, however, one can find an investment strategy that delivers a free lunch: an investment that offers an improved return with lower risk. In this chapter, we will see how investing in sectors with low correlations to one another has actually provided investors with above-average returns—even when factoring in risk or volatility.

I first got the idea to perform such a sector correlation analysis during a Standard & Poor's Investment Policy Committee meeting. Someone stated that "whenever technology stocks go down, health-care stocks go up." I wondered if this statement was true. My first inclination was to say, "No," as there is a lot of technology in health care— particularly with medical device and equipment companies. So I decided to check things out.

SECTOR RISKS AND RETURNS

I started by examining which sectors within the S&P 500 provided the best annual price returns, on average, since 1990. Figure 4.1 shows the average annual price changes for each of the 10 sectors in the S&P 500, their compound annual growth rates, volatility (as measured by the standard deviation of average annual returns) and risk-adjusted returns, or the average annual returns divided by the standard deviation.

High Price Returns Usually Mean High Volatility

Average Annual S&P 500 Sector Price Changes and Volatility, 1990–2007				
S&P 500 Sectors	**Average Annual Change**	**Compound Growth Rate**	**Standard Deviation**	**Risk-Adjusted Return**
Information Technology	15.6%	10.8%	33.4	0.47
Health Care	12.4%	10.1%	23.7	0.52
Energy	12.0%	11.0%	14.7	0.82
Financials	11.7%	9.5%	22.6	0.52
Industrials	10.2%	9.0%	16.0	0.64
Consumer Staples	10.1%	9.1%	15.1	0.67
S&P 500	**9.5%**	**8.2%**	**16.5**	**0.57**
Consumer Discretionary	9.4%	7.4%	20.8	0.45
Materials	7.8%	6.9%	13.7	0.56
Utilities	6.3%	4.2%	21.1	0.30
Telecommunications Services	5.8%	2.9%	24.4	0.24

Source: Standard & Poor's Equity Research
Past performance is no guarantee of future results.

We can clearly see that had someone invested in the S&P 500 Information Technology index 18 years ago, and left this investment alone, they would have experienced the highest average annual return of 15.6%, as compared with 9.5% for the S&P 500. They probably would have been thrilled, since Tech's average annual gain was more than 300 basis points (or 3 percentage points) above Health Care, the next-highest performer.

In fact, an investor might have been pretty happy had they invested in any of six sectors—IT, Health Care, Energy, Financials, Industrials, or Consumer Staples—since each posted returns that beat the average for the S&P 500. Only those who concentrated on the Utilities and Telecommunications Services sectors, and to a lesser extent the Consumer Discretionary and Materials areas, would have been disappointed.

Even when accounting for annual price fluctuations, as found in the Compound Growth Rate column, we see that the S&P 500 Information Technology sector performed exceedingly well, overtaken just recently by the S&P 500 Energy sector.

PAYING THE PRICE

Yet Tech investors had to pay a higher price, in a sense, for this above-average annual return in the form of increased annual price volatility. Specifically, while the S&P 500 had recorded a 16.5% standard deviation of annual returns since 1990, the Technology investor experienced a whopping 33.4% standard deviation. In other words, the volatility for the S&P 500 Information Technology sector was twice as great as the volatility for the S&P 500.

To better illustrate what this difference in volatility magnitude might mean, take a look at Figure 4.2, two charts that

FIGURE 4.2

If You Think the S&P is Volatile, Get a Load of Tech.

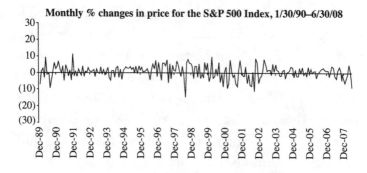

Monthly % changes in price for the S&P 500 Index, 1/30/90–6/30/08

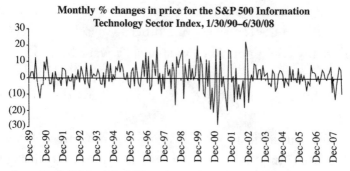

Monthly % changes in price for the S&P 500 Information Technology Sector Index, 1/30/90–6/30/08

75

Source: Standard & Poor's Equity Research
Past performance is no guarantee of future results.

show the monthly price change percentages for the S&P 500 and Information Technology sector from 1990 to 2007. Both charts have the same scale, so you can readily see that the monthly swings for the S&P 500 Information Technology sector were much greater than that for the overall market.

While the S&P 500 recorded an average monthly change of +0.7%, Tech's average gain was +1.2%. What's more, even though the highest and lowest monthly price swing for the S&P 500 was an unsettling +11.2% and −14.6%, respectively, Tech's results were nearly twice as bad, with a single-month advance of 22.0% and a one-month decline of 23.8%. In the end, you might say that Tech's chart of monthly volatility looks more like an EKG diagram!

At this point, one might logically ask, "Was this additional return worth the extra risk?" That obviously depends on the investor. Some could have weathered the extremely volatile annual returns, while others—myself included—probably could not. But I'm spoiled. I want both. I want the increased return offered by Tech, as well as the low volatility experienced by Materials. In other words, I want a free lunch.

How can someone get a free lunch on Wall Street? Diversification. And the way to get this free lunch isn't through the combining of just any two sectors. True diversification involves the pairing of uncorrelated sectors.

SMOOTHING THE SWINGS

Sectors are said to have low correlation when the price of one zigs, while the other zags. Over the long term, sectors with low correlations have recorded advances and declines at a different rate of pace, as if they each marched to the beat of a different drummer. Highly correlated sectors, on the other hand, ascended the staircase of price changes as if marching to the same beat.

Figure 4.3 shows the correlation coefficient of the rolling 12-month price changes for sectors in the S&P 500 since 1990. A reading of +1.0 represents perfect positive correlation. This means that when one sector rose, so did the other. Think of a Marine Corps drill team, always

FIGURE 4.3

Zeroing in on Zigs and Zags

Correlations of Monthly Price Changes, 1990–2007									
S&P 500 Sectors	**E**	**M**	**I**	**CD**	**CS**	**HC**	**F**	**IT**	**TS**	**U**
Energy	–	0.54	0.49	0.33	0.28	0.27	0.42	0.27	0.29	0.50
Materials	0.54	–	0.77	0.65	0.40	0.29	0.60	0.44	0.35	0.24
Industrials	0.49	0.77	–	0.79	0.50	0.45	0.73	0.62	0.50	0.34
Cons. Discretionary	0.33	0.65	0.79	–	0.46	0.40	0.72	0.66	0.54	0.19
Cons. Staples	0.28	0.40	0.50	0.46	–	0.66	0.59	0.17	0.30	0.35
Health Care	0.27	0.29	0.45	0.40	0.66	–	0.54	0.28	0.39	0.31
Financials	0.42	0.60	0.73	0.72	0.59	0.54	–	0.44	0.50	0.41
Info. Technology	0.27	0.44	0.62	0.66	0.17	0.28	0.44	–	0.48	0.05
Telecom. Services	0.29	0.35	0.50	0.54	0.30	0.39	0.50	0.48	–	0.23
Utilities	0.50	0.24	0.34	0.19	0.35	0.31	0.41	0.05	0.23	–
S&P 500	**0.52**	**0.68**	**0.87**	**0.86**	**0.56**	**0.59**	**0.81**	**0.79**	**0.66**	**0.35**

Source: Standard & Poor's Equity Research Services
Past performance is no guarantee of future results.

doing the exact thing in unison. A reading of -1.0, however, means perfectly negative correlation. Like Fred Astaire and Ginger Rogers, they each moved in opposite directions. When one went forward, the other stepped backward. A reading of 0.0 shows no correlation. Like cats, they pretty much do their own thing, regardless of what the other does.

Read the material in Figure 4.3 the way you would the mileage charts on old driving maps: look for the data point at the intersection of the row and the columns. For instance, the correlation coefficient for Consumer Discretionary and Industrials, which is boxed, is 0.79. This also happens to be the sector pair with the highest correlation of monthly price changes since 1990. On the other hand, the sector with the lowest correlation to Information Technology was Consumer Staples.

At this point, a sharp-eyed reader will instantly protest, "Hey, the Utilities sector actually has the lowest correlation with Technology." Technically, that person would be correct. But in this chapter, I will focus on exploiting the diversification benefits between the S&P 500 Information Technology and Consumer Staples sectors for two reasons.

First, when I created this investment strategy earlier this decade, Consumer Staples and Tech did have the lowest correlation among pairs. The Utilities/Tech relation has changed only in the past few years due to the explosive rise in energy prices, as most of utilities' unregulated businesses are energy-related.

Second, as you saw in Figure 4.1, the S&P 500 Utilities sector recorded the second-lowest average annual price gain since 1990. That's because investors typically purchase Utilities for their dividend yield, not price appreciation potential. And the same goes for Telecommunications Services companies, which posted the lowest average annual performance. As of the end of 2007, these two sectors sported the highest dividend yields of all 10 sectors in the S&P 500. Their dividend payments yielded more than 3.0% each, which is well above the average dividend yield for the S&P 500 as a whole, which was below 2.0%.

Therefore, since the investment strategies exploiting the Seven Rules of Wall Street focus on outperforming the S&P 500 on a price-appreciation basis, I am sticking with the Consumer Staples sector to be my low-correlation pair with the Information Technology sector.

PROFITING FROM THE PAIRING

Now I wondered what my compound annual growth rate and volatility would have been if I had exploited this low correlation between Consumer Staples and Information Technology. (Remember that the compound annual growth rate is the best measure to see how your portfolio would have performed over time.) So I created a portfolio containing 50% staples and 50% tech, which I rebalanced annually. I hoped that their dissimilar correlations would neutralize some of the annual volatility. And while I expected a lower standard deviation, I also anticipated a compound growth rate for this 50/50 portfolio to be somewhere in between the 10.8% for Information Technology and 9.1% for Consumer Staples.

What did I find? While I didn't scream, "It's alive!" the way Dr. Frankenstein did in the 1932 film classic, I can honestly say that I was pleasantly surprised by the results.

Figure 4.4 shows that from 1990 through 2007, the S&P 500 index recorded a compound annual growth rate of 8.2%, a standard deviation of 16.5%, and a risk-adjusted return of 0.50. The S&P 500 Information Technology sector, while posting the market-beating compound growth rate of 10.8%, also recorded a heart-thumping volatility reading of 33.4%, which was more than twice that for the overall market. As a result, it should come as no surprise that the risk-adjusted return for the Tech sector was lower than the market's at 0.32.

Yet the portfolio containing a 50% exposure to the S&P 500 Consumer Staples sector, and a 50% weighting in the S&P 500 Information Technology sector demonstrated two benefits.

FIGURE 4.4

Diversification Truly Is the Only Free Lunch on Wall Street

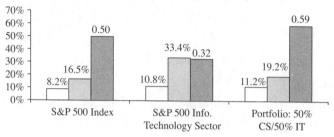

Compound Annual Growth Rates and Volatility, 12/31/90

☐ Compound Annual Growth Rate
☐ Standard Deviation
■ Risk-Adjusted Return

Source: Standard & Poor's Equity Research. Past performance is no guarantee of future results.

First, the compound annual growth rate for this 50/50 mix was not somewhere in between Tech's 10.8% compound growth rate and Consumer Staples' lower 9.1%, as I had expected. It was actually above both, at 11.2%! How could this be true? Answer: diversifying with sectors that have low correlations. That's how.

What's more, this 50/50 portfolio's higher compound growth rate was achieved with a substantially lower standard deviation, or volatility, than that registered by the Information Technology sector by itself. The volatility reading for the 50/50 portfolio was 19.2% versus 33.4% for Technology. As a result, the 50/50 portfolio scored a higher risk-adjusted return of 0.59 to the market's 0.50, despite the slightly higher standard deviation than the S&P 500's, and nearly twice Tech's risk-adjusted return of 0.32.

So, should history repeat itself (and there is no guarantee that it will), investors who have diversified portfolios of low correlated assets would likely receive higher absolute and risk-adjusted returns than they would had they invested in a single sector. In the case of the Free Lunch portfolio, a 50% exposure to each of the two uncorrelated sectors—Information Technology and Consumer Staples—rebalanced annually, may provide that outperformance in returns and volatility.

Who says there's no free lunch on Wall Street?

BEHAVIOR AND LONG-TERM OUTPERFORMANCE

I believe this investment strategy will continue to outperform in the years to come, so long as the equity market goes through cyclical periods of fear and greed. And I have no doubt it will.

During a bull market, investors typically gravitate toward the economically cyclical sectors. Investors anticipate that these groups will experience the greatest earnings growth. They therefore will likely see the biggest price rises. What's more, investors have traditionally regarded Information Technology as the poster child for cyclical earnings growth and share-price appreciation during bull market phases.

Yet the share prices for Consumer Staples companies—found in the food, beverage, tobacco, and household products industries—traditionally have held up best during challenging periods for equity market. That's because people will continue to eat, smoke, and drink, regardless of the outlook for the economy or corporate earnings. As a result, the demand for the products and services provided by Consumer Staples companies tends to remain fairly static during good times and bad.

While the same might be said for health-care companies, I believe the government's increasing efforts to regulate the Health Care sector to control costs as baby boomers age and face rising health-care costs could suppress some of this sector's defensive characteristics in the future.

Therefore, I believe that so long as the equity market maintains its cyclical dance between optimism and pessimism, investors will continuously rotate between cyclical (Information Technology) and defensive (Consumer Staples) sectors in an effort to beat the overall market.

BUILDING YOUR OWN FREE LUNCH PORTFOLIO

Assembling a Free Lunch portfolio, like developing a Sell in May portfolio, can be done easily using only two ETFs that mimic the price performances of the S&P 500 Consumer Staples and Information Technology sectors.

Let's use Figure 4.5 as a guide. Assume you have $30,000 that you plan to use to assemble a Free Lunch portfolio. Start by investing 50%, or $15,000, in the Consumer Staples Select Sector ETF (XLP). Invest the other 50%, or $15,000, in the Information Technology Select Sector ETF (XLK). It makes no difference where we are in the calendar year when you initiate this portfolio. Just split your holdings 50/50. The prices I used in Figure 4.5 were as of June 30, 2008.

At the end of each calendar year, rebalance the portfolio. By this I mean, should the Information Technology component of the portfolio have grown to, let's say, $18,000, while the Consumer Staples component have declined to $14,000, your overall portfolio would be worth $32,000. Since you want to have an equal amount ($16,000) in each component, you need to sell $2,000 worth of the XLK and purchase an additional $2,000 of

FIGURE 4.5

Creating Your Own Free Lunch Portfolio

Two S&P 500 Sectors	Free Lunch Portfolio		
	SPDR ETF Tickers	**Price**	**No. of Shares**
Consumer Staples	XLP	$27	556
Information Technology	XLK	$23	652

Source: Standard & Poor's Equity Research

the XLP. Now both the XLK and XLP components are worth $16,000, and represent 50% of this portfolio.

This annual rebalancing forces investors to take profits at the end of each year. It also requires them to reinvest in the prior year's underperformer, thus buying low and selling high—a principal tenet of long-term investing.

It's as simple as that.

TECHNOLOGY TECHNICALITY

There is one thing you should be aware of when using the Information Technology Select Sector ETF (XLK): it also contains Telecommunications Services companies. The S&P Telecommunications Services sector is very small. It represents about 3% of the total weighting of the S&P 500 and contains fewer than 10 companies. As a result, the creators of the Technology Select Sector ETF (XLK) chose to lump the Telecom issues in with the tech stocks. As a result, the performances you will receive by using the Information Technology Select Sector ETF (XLK) will differ from the performance for the S&P 500 Information technology sector itself. Therefore, you may want to consider using ETFs that are "purer" plays. Again, I encourage you to visit www.amex.com and www.nyse.com to research the composition of all technology-oriented sector-specific ETFs.

I hope you enjoy your free lunch.

Taking a buy-and-hold approach with sectors is like buying a Ferrari and then driving behind a school bus the rest of your life.

—SAM STOVALL

THERE'S ALWAYS A BULL MARKET SOMEPLACE

Have you ever been to Coney Island or to an arcade at an amusement park? There is a game—Whac-a-Mole—where you get points for bopping the mole that randomly, and swiftly, emerges from one of six holes. Sometimes I'm quick enough to whack him more than 50% of the time. Other times, I'm embarrassed to admit, he ends up snickering at me like the groundhog from the movie *Caddyshack*. Regardless of my success ratio, the game releases my aggressions.

I mention this Midway money-waster because poor players of this game remind me of equity investors who do not employ a time-tested trading discipline. Their actions are usually based on emotion. As a result, they keep missing the mole by hitting where he last was. With investing, they always seem to buy a stock just after its price has already popped up and is on its way down.

I bring up this game as a reminder that, whether the U.S. stock market is heading up or down, there is always a bull market someplace. There is always a handful of sectors and industries in the S&P 500 that pop up as outperformers. Some rise, others fall. What's more, these winners and losers constantly change.

Wouldn't it be nice to employ a portfolio strategy that allows you to "whack the mole" on a frequent basis? Wouldn't you like to find a strategy that leverages the power of momentum investing but also provides you with the opportunity to redirect your investment focus on a more frequent basis than once per year?

Welcome to Rule 5: There's Always a Bull Market Someplace. This chapter will teach you how to construct a time-tested, momentum-based portfolio for sectors or industries that is updated monthly—rather than only once or twice a year.

A MONTHLY WINNERS UPDATE

The four rules I have already shared with you—Let Your Winners Ride, As Goes January, Sell in May, and No Free Lunch—essentially are buy-and-hold investment techniques.

In other words, after you have identified the industries or sectors to purchase, you hold on to them for either six or 12 months. No changing your mind along the way. For the Sell in May rule, you hold on to your investments for six months. For the other three strategies, you hold on for 12 months.

Many investors have told me, however, that these approaches are just too static for them. They want not only more action but also to "go with the flow." They want to be able to adjust to changing market conditions month in and month out.

Investors frequently worry that frozen portfolios force them to purchase a sector or industry that is just about to decline in price, or miss out on an opportunity to buy into sectors or industries that are on the verge of experiencing a pickup in price performance.

There are others who are just impatient and want to play the trader by rotating into and out of sectors or industries on a fairly regular basis. I, too, have always felt that using sectors to employ a buy-and-hold technique was boring. It was like owning a Ferrari and then driving behind a school bus for the rest of your life.

Basically, investors who are unwilling to embrace these static-portfolio approaches have a fear of commitment—not to a spouse, but to a particular investment discipline. To them I say, don't worry about it. There is a rule for you, too.

89

As my hero, Popeye, always announced, "I yam what I yam, and that's all that I yam." And that's why I developed the There's Always a Bull Market Someplace portfolios.

SOME SECTORS ARE ALWAYS OUT FRONT

Have you ever noticed that, whether the equity markets are rising or falling, some sectors and industries outperform the overall market, either on an absolute or a relative basis? Obviously, these market leaders are experiencing their own mini-bull markets. What's more, they can be rising even though the overall equity market—such as the S&P 500— may either be in a bull-, flat-, or bear-market mode. Well, that's the rule we will focus on in this chapter: how to identify and profit from those areas that are exhibiting superior relative price performance.

I have done extensive backtesting on various momentum models in an effort to derive a monthly momentum-based approach to investing in sectors and industries. Many analysts and investors have volunteered to me that they invest based on trailing one-, three-, six-, or 12-month price performances. Since they can't all be right, I decided to do my own analysis.

I came to the conclusion that trailing 12-month price performance is the best selection technique when employed on a monthly basis. I arrived at this determination after taking into consideration compound annual growth rates, frequencies of beating the market, and portfolio turnover— or the number of times you replace your sector or industry holdings.

In other words, I believe a once-a-month look back at the prior 12 months of price changes offers the best overall results. In addition, I have found that you don't need to review the portfolio more than once a month. Actually, doing it more frequently than that just adds to your turnover, not to your performance.

A DYNAMIC "LET YOUR WINNERS RIDE"

This analysis basically confirms that you could have developed a dynamic, market-beating portfolio by leveraging the principals behind the Let Your Winners Ride rule. And all you need to do is reexamine your holdings based on their trailing 12-month price performances at the end of each month. You add industries to your portfolio as their relative price performance improves, and remove them when their trailing 12-month price advances begin to slow.

If you think that's too easy to be successful, take a look at the annual results for the S&P 500 and the two There's Always a Bull Market Someplace portfolios during the past 17 years.

As seen in Figure 5.1, the S&P 500 posted an average annual return of 10.4% since 1991. Not bad. Yet the There's Always a Bull Market Someplace portfolio for sectors recorded a 14.6% annual return. It beat the S&P 500 by an average of 420 basis points (or more than 4 percentage points) per year. Think you can top that? Well, get a load of the There's Always a Bull Market Someplace portfolio for industries, which posted an average annual performance of 22.3%. That was nearly twice the average gain for the S&P 500!

Now that I have your attention, let's get a little better acquainted with these portfolio approaches.

92

FIGURE 5.1

There's Always a Bull Market Someplace Portfolios Beat the Market

Average Annual Price Changes, 1991–2007

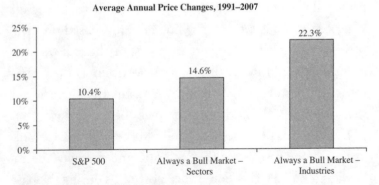

Source: Standard & Poor's Equity Research
Past performance is no guarantee of future results.

THERE'S ALWAYS A BULL MARKET SOMEPLACE FOR INDUSTRIES

In its simplest form, the There's Always a Bull Market Someplace portfolio for industries is merely a monthly update of the Let Your Winners Ride portfolio for industries. As you recall, this is a list of the 10 industries in the S&P 500 that exhibited the strongest trailing 12-month price performances. But rather than wait until the end of each year to update your top 10 holdings, you do so at the end of each month. Remove those industries that fell out of the top 10, and add those that entered the top 10. What could be simpler? Actually, the There's Always a Bull Market Someplace portfolio for sectors is simpler, but I'll get to that in a minute.

The intent of the There's Always a Bull Market Someplace portfolio for industries is to maintain an ownership of all industries that have had the highest trailing 12-month price performance. Your goal is to buy high but sell higher. In addition, the number of holdings never changes. This makes the management of the portfolio fairly straightforward.

A drawback to the There's Always a Bull Market Someplace portfolio for industries is turnover. The portfolio requires monthly fine-tuning. Since 1990, you would have added and subtracted an average of three industries per month. Two swaps a month was the most frequent occurrence. However, up to six swaps in a month occurred eight times since 1990. As you can see, this is a portfolio that experiences a fairly high rate of turnover. Like an active pet, it requires a lot of attention.

High turnover isn't the problem it used to be, however. Because of the existence of discount brokers and tax-deferred accounts such as individual retirement accounts (IRAs), the cost and tax consequence of employing a high-turnover technique is of less consequence than it was nearly 10 years ago. Plus, this opportunity to adjust your holdings once a month may be just what the doctor ordered for fidgety investors.

NON-ETF DRAWBACK

Remember, however, that creating your own There's Always a Bull Market Someplace portfolio for industries is a bit tricky. There are very few ETFs that mimic industries within the S&P 500. You, therefore, will need to select a company to serve as an industry's representative, or proxy. Again, you can select the individual representatives by choosing the largest company within each industry. You can also leverage S&P equity analysts' expertise by selecting each industry index's component stock that has the highest investment ranking.

If you want an even easier way to invest in rule number 5, keep reading.

ALWAYS A BULL MARKET FOR SECTORS

Some investors prefer to invest in ETFs rather than have to take the additional step of selecting an industry proxy. I fully understand the reasons for this. That's why I developed the There's Always a Bull Market Someplace portfolio for sectors.

In essence, the There's Always a Bull Market Someplace portfolio for sectors is merely a monthly update of the Let Your Winners Ride portfolio for sectors. This is a list of the three sectors in the S&P 500 that exhibited the strongest trailing 12-month price performance. But again, rather than wait until the end of each year to update your top three holdings, you do so at the end of each month. You remove those sectors that fell out of the top three, and add those that entered the top three. In other words, your portfolio will always consist of those three sectors that have had the highest trailing 12-month price performances.

See? I told you this was going to be simple. Not only is it simple, but it also works great! Check this out.

PERFORMANCE SUMMARIES

Let's take a look at how well these portfolios have performed over time. Figure 5.2 summarizes the average annual price changes, compound annual growth rates, standard deviations, risk-adjusted returns, frequencies of beating the S&P 500, and annual turnover. All data points are listed for the S&P 500 and the There's Always a Bull Market Someplace portfolios for sectors and industries.

As seen in Figure 5.2, the S&P 500 posted an average annual return of 10.4% from 1991 through 2007. Its compound annual growth rate was 9.2%. It also recorded a standard deviation of 16.0. Its risk-adjusted return (based on its average annual return), therefore, was 0.65. Since the S&P 500 can't beat itself, there is an "NA" in the "Frequency of Beating the S&P 500" column. You'll notice that I added an "Annual Turnover" column. This shows how active an investor must be to maintain this portfolio. The number of companies being added to or removed from the S&P 500 amounts to only 5% per year. That's equivalent to replacing 25 companies per year.

In the case of the There's Always a Bull Market Someplace portfolio for industries, the average annual price change was an astounding 22.3%, or nearly 10 full percentage points above that for the S&P 500. More important, its compound annual growth rate was 20.1%, which was greater than twice the compound rate for the market.

Yes, the There's Always a Bull Market Someplace portfolio for industries saw higher volatility, with a standard deviation of 24.1 versus 16.0 for the "500," but I think it was well worth it, since the risk-adjusted return was 0.93.

FIGURE 5.2

Beating the Market with There's Always a Bull Market Someplace Portfolios

	There's Always A Bull Market Someplace Portfolios, 1991–2007					
Portfolio	Average Annual Return	Compound Growth Rate	Standard Deviation	Risk-Adjusted Return	Frequency of Beating S&P 500	Annual Turn-over
S&P 500	10.4%	9.2%	16.0	0.65	NA	5%
There's Always a Bull Market Portfolios						
– Industries	22.3%	20.1%	24.1	0.93	71%	298%
– Sectors	14.6%	13.4%	16.5	0.89	76%	225%

Source: Standard & Poor's Equity Research
Past performance is no guarantee of future results.

That was substantially above that for the overall market. In addition, this portfolio's annual results beat the S&P 500's more than 70% of the time.

But take a look at the annual turnover: nearly 300%. This means that you engaged in 30 swaps during the entire year. In other words, you turned over your portfolio of 10 industries three times. That's a lot. But don't sweat it if you trade within a tax-deferred account, use a discount broker and thrive on the monthly attention.

The results for the There's Always a Bull Market Someplace portfolio for sectors are similar to those for industries, but muted. The average annual return of 14.6% was more than 400 basis points above the market's. The compound rate of growth was also more than 4 percentage points above the S&P 500's. It produced a more favorable risk-adjusted return. It also beat the market more than three out of every four years. Its turnover, however, was still relatively high.

One plus for the There's Always a Bull Market Someplace portfolio for sectors is that it will be a lot easier to mimic the results on a sector level. Let's face it, you don't have to worry about finding an appropriate single-stock proxy for each industry.

TAKEAWAYS

I believe the most important takeaway from this analysis is that sometimes it doesn't pay to try to be Fred Astaire—you are better off just letting the market lead. And that's exactly what this rule endorses. Instead of picking sectors, industries, or stocks by trying to forecast where we are in the economic cycle, projecting which company will win a government contract, or guessing which way the dollar will fluctuate, let the market tell you where to invest your money.

In addition, investors usually have been too quick to take profits by selling out of a stock too soon that still has a long way to go to the upside. What's more, these same investors usually hold on to a losing stock too long, saying to themselves, "I'll get out once I break even or recoup a portion of my loss." With Rule 5, There's Always a Bull Market

Someplace, you can let the market tell you which areas to buy into and when to sell out.

INVESTOR BEHAVIOR MAY MAINTAIN SUCCESS

Granted, past performance is no guarantee of future results. But just as with the Let Your Winners Ride rule, investors will usually be very happy to brag about a stock that they own that has recently hit a 52-week high, enticing others to mimic their successes and keep the trend intact. Conversely, whoever owns a stock that recently hit a 52-week low will likely dump the dog when it shows any sign of improving.

BUILDING YOUR OWN THERE'S ALWAYS A BULL MARKET SOMEPLACE PORTFOLIO

How can you put together your own There's Always a Bull Market Someplace portfolio for sectors and industries? Easy. At the beginning of each month, subscribers to Standard & Poor's www.spoutlook.com service can retrieve the S&P Sector Scorecard, which shows the 12-month price performance rankings for the sectors and industries in the S&P 500. You want to identify the 10 industries and three sectors with the best trailing 12-month price performances. You can also go to www.sectorspdr.com to find out, free of charge, the price performances for their nine-sector ETFs.

CREATING YOUR OWN THERE'S ALWAYS A BULL MARKET SOMEPLACE PORTFOLIO FOR SECTORS

Look at Figure 5.3. Assume you have $30,000 that you plan to use in order to put together a There's Always a Bull Market Someplace portfolio for sectors. One-third would be invested in each of the three sectors that posted the best performances in the prior 12 months.

For instance, as of June 30, 2008, the three sectors with the highest trailing 12-month price performances were the S&P 500 Energy, Materials, and Utilities sectors. If, on July 1, 2008, you chose to invest in the Select Sector SPDRs ETFs that mimic these S&P 500 sectors, you would have purchased an equal dollar amount of the Energy Select Sector ETF (XLE), the Materials Select Sector ETF (XLB), and the Utilities Select Sector ETF (XLU).

FIGURE 5.3

Creating Your Own There's Always a Bull Market Someplace Portfolio for Sectors

Allocating Your $30,000			
Top 3 S&P 500 Sectors	**SPDR ETF Ticker**	**Price**	**No. of Shares**
Energy	XLE	$88	114
Materials	XLB	$42	238
Utilities	XLU	$41	244

Source: Standard & Poor's Equity Research

You would then leave this portfolio untouched until August 1, 2008, when you would look to see which three of the 10 sectors in the S&P 500 had the highest trailing 12-month price performances. If the S&P 500 Materials sector had been replaced by the S&P 500 Consumer Staples sector, you would sell your shares in the Materials Select Sector ETF (XLB) and use the proceeds to purchase shares in the Consumer Staples Select Sector ETF (XLP).

SECTORS ARE EASIER THAN INDUSTRIES

Creating your own There's Always a Bull Market Someplace portfolio for industries is a bit trickier than developing a sector portfolio, since there are very few ETFs that mimic industries within the S&P 500. What I suggest is selecting a company to serve as an industry's representative, or proxy. I again recommend leveraging S&P equity analysts' expertise by selecting each industry index's component stock that had the highest investment ranking as of the end of each month.

Subscribers can do the same thing by signing on to www.spoutlook.com and performing a stock screen, searching for the companies within each industry that have the highest S&P STARS (buy, sell, or hold ranking). If you find that there is more than one stock with the highest investment ranking, select the issue with the largest market cap. All industries should have one representative company, regardless of their S&P STARS.

You now have all the information you need to develop your own There's Always a Bull Market Someplace portfolio. Good luck.

LET S&P DO THE WORK FOR YOU

I developed a variation of There's Always a Bull Market Someplace portfolio for industries, and have been sharing it with S&P clients for more than 10 years. I call it the Industry Momentum portfolio, and it is available on several S&P's electronic delivery services, including www.spout look.com.

I introduced this variation of There's Always a Bull Market Someplace portfolio for industries in order to reduce annual turnover. The buy and sell parameters of the There's Always a Bull Market Someplace portfolio for industries have been loosened to allow an industry to experience a bit of profit taking without being removed from the portfolio. Quite simply, I select those industries that have trailing 12-month price performances in the top 10% of the universe of industries, and remove them when their trailing price performances fall out of the top 30%. That's the only variation from the There's Always a Bull Market Someplace for industries concept.

Because the S&P 500 has approximately 130 industries in it, no fewer than 13 industries will be in my Industry Momentum portfolio during any month. And since I don't sell an industry until its trailing 12-month price performance has fallen out of the top 30%, the Industry Momentum portfolio has had an average of 18 industries since inception in April 1999. For some investors, this variable number of industries may be a limitation. But its compound annual growth rate and frequency of beating the S&P 500 make up for this limitation, in my opinion. Plus, at 117%, the average annual turnover for the Industry Momentum portfolio is dramatically lower than the turnover for the There's Always a Bull Market Someplace portfolio for industries.

Again, because of the lack of ETFs to mimic these industries (ETFs had not been invented when I started this portfolio), I select the stock in the industry index with the highest S&P STARS to serve as an industry proxy. The tie goes to the stock with the largest market value. I'm quite happy to report that the performance has been impressive, as seen in Figure 5.4. Of course, past performance is no guarantee of future results. From April 30, 1999, through December 31, 2007, the Industry Momentum portfolio has beaten the S&P 500 in eight of nine years, and posted an average annual return of 12.7% to the S&P 500 average annual advance of only 2.1%.

FIGURE 5.4

Let S&P Do the Work for You

	S&P's Industry Momentum Portfolio, 4/30/99–12/31/07	
	Annual % Changes (No Dividends)	
Years	**S&P's Industry Momentum Portfolio**	**S&P 500 Index**
1999	38.1%	10.1%
2000	−2.4%	−10.1%
2001	−5.6%	−13.0%
2002	−15.2%	−23.4%
2003	44.6%	26.4%
2004	16.1%	9.0%
2005	17.1%	3.0%
2006	3.3%	13.6%
2007	18.4%	3.5%
Average	**12.7%**	**2.1%**

Source: Standard & Poor's Equity Research
Past performance is no guarantee of future results.

So go ahead. Create your own There's Always a Bull Market Someplace portfolio. Or, let S&P do it for you. Either way, now at least you can enter the fast lane by pulling out from behind that slow, yellow school bus.

You have undertaken to cheat me. I won't sue you, for the law is too slow. I will ruin you.

—Cornelius Vanderbilt

DON'T GET MAD—
GET EVEN!

Do you remember the very old—and very corny—joke:

> "Where does an 800 pound gorilla sit?"
> "Anywhere he wants to!"

I think the person who came up with that joke may also have been involved with creating market-capitalization-weighted indexes. Capitalization is computed by multiplying the number of common shares outstanding by the share price. As a result, some companies are larger than others. In addition, the price action of the companies that have the largest market-capitalization accounts for a greater impact on the index's overall price performance than do those of smaller companies. And since some companies are so large, they represent the lion's share (or 800-pound-gorilla's share) of that industry index's price performance.

COMPOSITION OF THE S&P 500

Before I dive any further into the rule Don't Get Mad, Get Even, I think I should give you a little bit of background into the S&P 500 index, the world's most widely followed benchmark of U.S. large-company stocks. Not surprisingly, there are 500 stocks in this exclusively U.S. large-cap equity index. This index was created in 1957 from a 233-stock index that had been in existence since 1923. Its purpose is to serve as a proxy for the entire U.S. large-capitalization stock universe. It is not a portfolio that attempts to guess which sectors, industries, or stocks will be the best performers in the coming months or years. It attempts to be an accurate "snapshot" of the U.S. large-company equity market at that particular point in time. What's more, it is not simply the 500 largest companies found on U.S. stock exchanges. S&P's Index Committee assembled a comprehensive set of sectors and industries first, and then selected the most appropriate large-cap companies to represent these sectors and industries.

Large cap—like mid cap and small cap—refers to the size of the typical stock found within the benchmark, or the market that this overall index is attempting to emulate. Capitalization is computed by multiplying the number of common shares outstanding by the share price. For instance, on April 30, 2008, Exxon Mobil Corp. (XOM) was the largest company in the S&P 500 index. It had a market cap of $499 billion (5.35 billion shares x $93.07 per share).

HOW BIG IS BIG CAP; HOW SMALL IS SMALL CAP?

Typically, a company is called large cap if its capitalization is above $4.0 billion, while a small-cap company is $1.5 billion or less in size. A mid-cap stock is anything in between. However, there is no industry standard for what constitutes large- and small-cap thresholds. The average market cap of companies in the S&P 500 is $24.13 billion, whereas the average market caps for the S&P MidCap 400 and S&P SmallCap 600 indexes are $2.73 billion and $0.83 billion, respectively.

Those 500 companies in the S&P 500 are assembled into 130 industries and 10 sectors. Companies that sell similar products or services are assigned to a particular industry. For example, Coke and Pepsi make nonalcoholic beverages and therefore are assigned to the S&P 500 Soft Drinks Industry index.

Industries, on the other hand, that provide similar services and are affected in like ways by economic events or legislative/regulatory considerations are assigned to one of 10 sectors. Soft drink companies, as well as brewers, household products, and tobacco companies, are assigned to the S&P Consumer Staples sector index. More information about the S&P 500 can be found at www.standardandpoors.com in the area called "Indices."

WHEN DOES 10% EQUAL 50%?

When dealing with the market-cap-weighted S&P 500, the top 50 stocks—which represent 10% of the number of companies in the S&P 500—represent close to 50% of the market value of that index. As of the end of April 2008, the five largest companies in the S&P 500—ExxonMobil, General Electric, AT&T Corp., Microsoft, and Chevron—accounted for nearly 12% of the total market value for the entire S&P 500. What's more, only about 10% of the companies in the S&P 500—the largest 55 companies—accounted for 50% of the market value for that index. In other words, the price performance of these 55 stocks explained 50% of the price move for the S&P 500. The same goes for earnings. That's unfair, you might say, downright undemocratic even! But it's true.

When market-cap-weighted indexes are initiated, everything starts out equal. Over time, however, as some stocks fluctuate in price or alter the number of shares through secondary offerings and stock splits, their market value changes. The same goes for portfolios. Twenty years ago, you might have purchased an equal dollar amount of five different stocks, but today each of these stocks most likely represents a varying percentage of your portfolio's total value.

WHEN DOES 45% EQUAL 10%?

The 14 smallest companies in the S&P 500, on the other hand, which included Ambac Financial Group, Brunswick Corp., Dillard's, Jones Apparel, Liz Claiborne, OfficeMax, and Unisys, each accounted for only 0.1% (one-tenth of 1%) of the total market value for the "500." In fact, more than 225 companies in the S&P 500 accounted for less than 10% of the overall market value. As a result, they had only a negligible impact on the index's price and earnings-per-share performances.

At times, this market-cap favoritism has led to sector dominance that has resulted in devastating results to the index as a whole—and individual investors' portfolios in return—that has taken years to recover. Three examples of unhealthy "sector swelling" come to mind: Energy in the early 1980s, Information Technology in the late 1990s, and Financials in the late 2000s.

The sector bubble that many investors remember was the swelling of the Information Technology sector's market value to nearly 34% of the S&P 500 in August 2000, after starting the decade of the 1990s at less than 6%.

The subsequent 82% decline in the value of the S&P 500 Information Technology sector from March 24, 2000, through October 9, 2002, resulted in its market value being cut by more than 60% to 12.7%, and causing the S&P 500 to still be below its all-time high of 1,527 by more than 25% five years after the March 2000 peak. In fact, as I write this book in mid–2008, the S&P 500 Information Technology sector index's price is still 61% below its March 24, 2000, price level.

When these sector bubbles burst, because of the enormous proportion of their overall benchmark, they usually bring the S&P 500 down with it. "That's just not fair," you might say, particularly if you spotted this imbalance early on and reduced or eliminated your exposure to this sector, since your portfolio took it on the chin anyway. So what's an investor to do? As I said at the beginning of this chapter, "Don't get mad—get even." And that's exactly what I will show you how to do. I will show you how to avoid the effects of a market-cap-weighted index.

EQUALLY WEIGHTED COMPANIES

This disparity of single-stock influence caused many investors to ask S&P to develop an equally weighted S&P 500 index. The favorable long-term performance of smaller-cap companies, as well as their lower correlation with large-cap issues during the 2000–2002 mega-meltdown, probably also helped fan the interest in an equally weighted S&P 500 index. Since it was created on December 31, 1994, the S&P SmallCap 600 index has risen a cumulative 320% through May 30, 2008, versus a 205% advance for the S&P 500 index. In addition, it declined in only one year during the 2000–2002 bear market, falling 15% in 2002. The S&P 500, on the other hand, fell 10%, 13%, and 23% in 2000, 2001, and 2002, respectively. S&P's Index Committee responded by developing an index made up of the 500 companies in the original S&P 500, but with each company having a fixed one-fifth of 1%, or 0.20% (500 x 0.20 = 100), weighting within this equally weighted benchmark. Although this index was created in mid-decade, its history dates back to December 31, 1989.

113

To clarify the concept of an equally weighted S&P 500 index, the stock Big Lots (BIG) ended up having the same weighting as "Big Blue" (IBM), IBM's nickname. In the market-cap-weighted S&P 500, Big Blue, which as of April 30, 2008, was the eighth largest company, at $179 billion, had a market capitalization that was 70 times as large as Big Lots' $2.53 billion, number 471 in the S&P 500. Under the equally weighted system, both Big Lots and Big Blue are the same size, along with the 498 remaining companies in the S&P 500. Has it been worth the effort? Take a look at Figure 6.1 and judge for yourself.

Figure 6.1 compares annual price performances for the market-cap-weighted S&P 500 index with the equally

FIGURE 6.1

The Equally Weighted Index Has Trounced the Cap-Weighted Index

	Annual % Changes of Market-Cap and Equally Weighted S&P 500				
	S&P 500		Equally Weighted Beat Cap-Weighted?	Russell 2000/ S&P SC 600 Indexes	Small Caps Beat Large Caps?
	Cap-Weighted	Equally Weighted			
1990	−6.6%	−14.7%	No	−21.5%	No
1991	26.3%	31.7%	Yes	43.7%	Yes
1992	4.5%	12.7%	Yes	16.4%	Yes
1993	7.1%	12.5%	Yes	17.0%	Yes
1994	−1.5%	−1.6%	No	−3.2%	No
1995	34.1%	28.9%	No	28.6%	No
1996	20.3%	16.5%	No	20.1%	No
1997	31.0%	26.7%	No	24.5%	No
1998	26.7%	10.4%	No	−2.1%	No
1999	19.5%	10.2%	No	11.5%	No
2000	−10.1%	7.6%	Yes	11.0%	Yes
2001	−13.0%	−1.9%	Yes	5.7%	Yes
2002	−23.4%	−19.4%	Yes	−15.3%	Yes
2003	26.4%	38.7%	Yes	37.5%	Yes
2004	9.0%	15.2%	Yes	21.6%	Yes
2005	3.0%	6.4%	Yes	6.7%	Yes
2006	13.6%	14.0%	Yes	14.1%	Yes
2007	3.5%	0.0%	No	−4.5%	No
Average	9.5%	10.8%	56%	11.8%	56%
Risk (SD):	16.5	15.1		17.0	
Rtn/Risk:	0.57	0.71		0.69	

Source: Standard & Poor's Equity Research; Russell, Inc.
Past performance is no guarantee of future results.

114

weighted S&P 500 index from December 31, 1989, through December 31, 2007. Also shown is a column indicating whether the equally weighted index's annual price change was higher than that for the market-cap-weighted index. From these three columns, we see that the equally weighted index posted an average return of 10.8%, versus the cap-weighted's 9.5% return. In addition, we see that the equally weighted index beat the cap-weighted index 56% of the time.

In other words, over the past 18 years, the equally weighted S&P 500 posted an average annual return that beat the cap-weighted index by an average of 130 basis points (1.3 percentage points) per year, and posted superior results 56% of the time. At this point you might be saying to yourself, "Hey, I like getting even!" But if you are like the typical New Yorker, you might now be wondering "Okay, what's the catch? Did my annual volatility (standard deviation) skyrocket, or what?"

HIGHER RETURNS, LOWER RISK

Surprisingly, despite the equally weighted index's superior annual return, its risk or volatility (as indicated by the standard deviation of annual returns) was 15.1, which was lower than the cap-weighted index's 16.5. Needless to say, the risk-adjusted return ratio (return divided by risk, where a higher number is better) for the equally weighted index was greater than that for the cap-weighted index. Yes, here again, you could have gotten something for nothing, in the form of increased performance without an increase in volatility.

One reason for this improved risk-adjusted return is the even distribution of weight. In other words, since all companies have an equal weighting within the index, they will each have an equal impact on the index's price performance. This even distribution of weight may stop a sector index from "tipping over" due to the undue influence by a particular industry, much like an evenly loaded cargo ship will prevent it from tipping.

For instance, on April 30, 2001, the pharmaceuticals industry—which was one of six industries in the market-cap-weighted S&P 500 Health Care sector index—represented 75% of the cap-weighted Health Care sector's overall weighting. Yet from April 30, 2001, until November 30, 2005, when the industry's influence had fallen to 47% as a result of high-profile patented drugs coming off patent and thin new-drug pipelines, the S&P Pharmaceuticals index declined 35% in price. Even though you might have been encouraged by the investment prospects for smaller components in this sector, such as biotechnology, medical devices, or managed care, which jumped 32%, 45%, and a whopping 210%, respectively, the overall cap-weighted Health Care sector fell 8%. As a result, your overall performance was more closely aligned with the pharmaceuticals' decline than the others' advances.

SMALL-COMPANY INFLUENCE

The column labeled "Russell 2000 / S&P SC 600 Indexes" in Figure 6.1 shows the annual price performances for the Russell 2000 small-cap index from 1990 to 1994 and the S&P SmallCap 600 index from 1995 to 2007. I use both indexes, since S&P's small-cap index was not introduced until the end of 1994. Both of these are recognized small-company, or small-cap, benchmarks.

The final column in Figure 6.1 shows the frequency with which the small-cap indexes beat the cap-weighted S&P 500. As you can see, the small-cap benchmarks beat the large-cap S&P 500 in 56% of the years since 1990. Interestingly, the equally weighted index also beat the cap-weighted index during the exact same years that the small-cap benchmark did, and recorded the same percentage of years beating the cap-weighted S&P 500. These similar performances indicate that the equally weighted index's outperformance was most likely the result of the small caps' tendency to outperform large caps.

RISING RISK-ADJUSTED RETURNS

If the small-cap effect helped improve the performance and risk-adjusted return for the overall S&P 500, could an equally weighted approach also benefit the underlying sectors? Take a look at Figure 6.2, which compares the sectors in the Equally Weighted S&P 500 index with the sectors in the Market-Cap-Weighted S&P 500 index. Comparisons were made between representation within each index, compound annual price growth rates from December 31, 1989 through December 31, 2007, standard deviation of annualized price returns, and risk-adjusted return ratio.

FIGURE 6.2

Equally Weighted Sectors Typically Produced Higher Risk-Adjusted Returns

	Cap- and Equally Weighted S&P 500 Weightings, Performances, and Volatility, 1990–2007							
	Equally Weighted				Market-Cap.-Weighted			
Index & Sectors	Weight in S&P 500	Compound Growth Rate	Standard Deviation	Risk-Adj. Return	Weight in S&P 500	Compound Growth Rate	Standard Deviation	Risk-Adj. Return
S&P 500	NA	**9.8%**	**15.1**	**0.65**	NA	**8.2%**	**16.5**	**0.50**
Consumer Discretionary	17.0%	7.8%	18.7	0.42	8.7%	7.4%	20.8	0.36
Consumer Staples	8.5%	9.6%	13.6	0.71	11.8%	9.1%	15.1	0.60
Energy	6.7%	11.4%	21.8	0.52	13.2%	11.0%	14.7	0.75
Financials	17.8%	11.4%	24.0	0.47	15.8%	9.5%	22.6	0.42
Health Care	11.7%	13.5%	20.4	0.66	12.8%	10.1%	23.7	0.43
Industrials	10.9%	9.2%	15.8	0.59	11.4%	9.0%	16.0	0.56
Info. Technology	13.7%	12.6%	34.6	0.36	16.0%	10.8%	33.4	0.32
Materials	6.0%	8.0%	15.8	0.51	3.6%	6.9%	13.7	0.50
Telecom Services	1.9%	6.3%	28.3	0.22	3.2%	2.9%	24.4	0.12
Utilities	5.9%	5.6%	20.4	0.27	3.5%	4.2%	21.1	0.20

Source: Standard & Poor's Equity Research
Past performance is no guarantee of future results.

REPOSITIONING OF SECTOR WEIGHTS

As a result of equally weighting all of the companies in the S&P 500, the overall representation that each sector has within the broader benchmark has also changed. The equally weighted Consumer Discretionary, Materials, and Utilities sectors have seen the greatest percentage increase in weighting, or representation, while the Consumer Staples, Energy, and Telecommunications Services sectors have shown the largest reductions in representation. Finally, as of December 31, 2007, the Financials sector was the largest sector within the equally weighted S&P 500. In the market-capitalization-weighted S&P 500, the Information Technology sector was the largest.

IMPROVED COMPOUND GROWTH RATES

As Figure 6.2 reveals, all 10 equally weighted sectors posted compound annual growth rates (no dividends included) that were superior to the growth rates of their cap-weighted counterparts. In particular, the equally weighted Health Care, Information Technology, and Materials sectors showed the greatest improvements in comparative performances.

ELEVATED RISK-ADJUSTED RETURNS

Interestingly, five equally weighted sectors posted standard deviations that were equal to or less than their cap-weighted peers. The equally weighted Energy sector recorded a much higher standard deviation than the cap-weighted counterpart. Financials, Information Technology, and Materials recorded slightly higher volatility. But when you look at returns in conjunction with volatility, eight of the 10 equally weighted sectors posted risk-adjusted returns superior to their cap-weighted siblings. It was only the cap-weighted Energy and Industrials sectors that posted better risk-adjusted returns than their equally weighted equivalents. I can only guess that this tipping of the results had something to do with ExxonMobil and General Electric, which are mega-cap components in the Energy and Industrials sectors, respectively. Each stock represents more than 20% of the cap weighting of their sector, and sports a below-market beta. Beta is a relative level of volatility. It shows how much a stock fluctuates in comparison with the broader market.

EQUALLY WEIGHTED AND CAP-WEIGHTED ETFs

The S&P 500's 10 equally and market-capitalization-weighted sectors are assigned to nine ETFs. In the cap-weighted universe of ETFs, the Telecommunications Services sector was teamed up with the Information Technology sector. In the equally weighted universe of ETFs, the Telecommunications Services sector was teamed up with the Utilities sector. Because of the small market value and limited number of companies in the S&P 500 Telecommunications Services index, the companies that created the ETFs chose to combine Telecommunications with another sector. State Street Bank and Trust Company, the creator of the cap-weighted ETFs decided to lump Telecommunications with Technology (www.sectorspdr. com). Rydex Investments, creator of the equally weighted sector ETFs, elected to combine Telecommunications with Utilities (www.rydexinvestments.com). Additional information on these and other ETFs can be found on the American Stock Exchange's Web site: www.amex.com. Figure 6.3 lists the ticker symbols for the nine equally weighted and market-capitalization-weighted ETFs.

FIGURE 6.3

Equally Weighted and Cap-Weighted Sector ETFs

S&P 500 Sector ETFs and Ticker Symbols		
	ETF Ticker Symbols	
S&P 500 and its Sectors	**Rydex Equally Weighted**	**Select Sector SPDR Cap-Weighted**
Consumer Discretionary	RCD	XLY
Consumer Staples	RHS	XLP
Energy	RYE	XLE
Financials	RYF	XLF
Health Care	RYH	XLV
Industrials	RGI	XLI
Information Technology	RYT	–
Info. Tech./Telecom. Svcs.	–	XLK
Materials	RTM	XLB
Utilities	–	XLU
Utilities/Telecom. Svcs.	RYU	–
S&P 500	**RSP**	**SPY**

Source: Standard & Poor's Index Services

TAKEAWAYS

So what should an investor take away from all of this? Three things.

First, if you are a buy-and-hold investor who is looking to neutralize the influence of cap size in your portfolio, and take advantage of the historical outperformance of smaller-cap stocks over larger-cap ones, then you should invest in the equally weighted S&P 500 ETF. Should history repeat itself (and there's no guarantee that it will) over the long run, you too should experience an improvement in both your annual compound growth rate and risk-adjusted return.

Second, you might want to rotate between the equally weighted and market-cap-weighted S&P 500 indexes. The equally weighted S&P 500, like the small-cap indexes, will likely outperform the cap-weighted index periodically. As a result, you may choose to gravitate toward the equally weighted S&P 500 when you believe smaller-cap stocks are likely to outperform other stocks. Conversely, you may choose to rotate toward the cap-weighted S&P 500 when you believe large caps will have their day in the sun.

In both examples, please remember that past performance is no guarantee of future results. There is no assurance that the equally weighted S&P 500 will continue to beat the market-weighted S&P 500 by such a wide margin and frequency in the years ahead. But if you believe small-cap stocks will continue to post superior long-term results, then an equal-weighted approach might be the way to go. Also, an equal-weighted approach will allow the smaller-weighted industries to have a greater say in the earnings and price performance of the overall sector.

The third takeaway is the most important, in my opinion. It is the extra octane an investor receives when substituting equally weighted sectors for market-cap-weighted sectors in the portfolios discussed in this book. The Summary, Ranking the Rules, summarizes the performances, volatility, and frequencies of outperformance for each of the Seven Rules of Wall Street, using market-cap-weighted and equally weighted sector indexes. How you implement the rule Don't Get Mad—Get Even is just as simple as the ways you implement the other rules.

123

ASSEMBLING YOUR DON'T GET MAD PORTFOLIOS

The process for developing the Don't Get Mad portfolios will be the same as for each rule already discussed in this book. The only change is that you will substitute the equally weighted sector ETF for the cap-weighted sector ETF. All portfolios will invest the same $30,000.

Equally Weighted Let Your Winners Ride Portfolio

One-third would be invested in each of the three equally weighted sector ETFs that posted the best performances in the prior calendar year. The 2008 Winners portfolio consisted of the equally weighted S&P 500 Energy, Health Care, and Industrials sectors. They posted the best price performances of all sectors during 2007.

Equally Weighted As Goes January Portfolio

One-third would be invested in each of the three equally weighted sector ETFs that posted the best performances during January. The 2008–2009 January Barometer portfolio for sectors consisted of the equally weighted S&P 500 Consumer Discretionary, Financials, and Health Care sectors. They posted the best price performances of all sectors during January 2008.

Equally Weighted Sell in May Portfolio

Substitute the equally weighted S&P 500 Consumer Staples sector ETF for the cap-weighted Consumer Staples sector ETF. If you prefer Health Care, substitute the equally weighted S&P 500 Health Care sector ETF for the cap-weighted Health Care sector ETF. If you choose to hedge your bets, invest one-half in the equally weighted S&P 500 Consumer Staples ETF and the other half in the equally weighted S&P 500 Health Care ETF.

Equally Weighted No Free Lunch Portfolio

Substitute the equally weighted S&P 500 Consumer Staples and Technology ETFs for the market-cap-weighted S&P 500 Consumer Staples and Technology ETFs. What could be easier?

Equally Weighted Always a Bull Market Someplace Portfolio

125

Every month, maintain a one-third holding in the three equally weighted S&P 500 ETFs with the highest trailing 12-month price performance.

PRACTICAL EXAMPLES

Figure 6.4 gives a practical example of creating your own equally weighted S&P 500 sector portfolios using the same initial investment of $30,000.

You now have all the information you need to develop your own Don't Get Mad, Get Even portfolios. So, get going!

FIGURE 6.4

Creating Your Own Equally Weighted S&P 500 Sector Portfolios

Equally Weighted Portfolios	Rydex ETF Tickers	Price	No. of Shares
Let Your Winners Ride Portfolio			
Energy	RYE	$59	169
Health Care	RYH	$54	185
Industrials	RGI	$51	196
As Goes January Portfolio			
Energy	RYE	$59	169
Materials	RTM	$51	196
Utilities	RYU	$53	189
Sell in May Portfolio			
Consumer Staples	RHS	$50	600
Health Care	RYH	$54	556
1/2 Staples and	RHS	$50	300
1/2 Health Care	RYH	$54	278
No Free Lunch Portfolio			
1/2 Staples and	RHS	$50	300
1/2 Technology	RYT	$42	357
Always a Bull Market Someplace Portfolio			
Energy	RYE	$59	169
Materials	RTM	$51	196
Utilities	RYU	$53	189

The table above is titled: **Dividing a Hypothetical $30,000 Among Equally Weighted Portfolio Members**

126

Source: Standard & Poor's Equity Research

You don't tug on Superman's cape.

—JIM CROCE

DON'T FIGHT THE FED

The musicians Jim Croce singing "You Don't Mess Around with Jim," Jimmy Dean reciting the ballad of "Big Bad John," or even the Olympics crooning about "Big Boy Pete," could easily have been singing about the approach that investors should take with the U.S. Federal Reserve Bank. Quite simply: "you don't fight the Fed."

I have frequently been asked, "What is the one thing an investor should monitor in order to gauge the health of the economy and the direction of the stock market?"

My response is "interest rates." The mandate of the Federal Reserve is twofold: to promote economic growth and to keep inflation under control. In other words, make capital (money) abundant enough so that consumers and companies will be willing to borrow money in order to expand and improve their overall quality of life. But, at the same time, be vigilant about the potential increase in inflation, as a result of too many people and companies chasing after a more limited supply of goods or services. And should inflation begin to speed up, as Fed chairman William McChesney Martin once said, the central bank's responsibility is to "take away the punch bowl just when the party starts getting interesting."

INTEREST RATES AND THE ECONOMY

Think of it this way. If the economy were a car, the Fed's responsibility as a driver would be to maintain a safe speed. If the Fed wanted to speed things up, then they would step on the gas by lowering interest rates. To slow things down, however, the Fed would need to tap or even slam on the brakes by raising interest rates and reducing the availability of capital.

The biggest challenge for the Fed is that our economy isn't a little red sports car that reacts nimbly to the application of the gas pedal or the brakes. Instead, the economy is more like a supertanker whose response time is remarkably slow. It usually takes between six and 12 months for the economy to feel the stimulation effects of lower rates. It also takes quite some time for the economy to slow down as a result of higher rates.

INTEREST RATES, GDP, AND EARNINGS

So how do the raising and lowering of interest rates affect stock prices? Investors buy stocks because they "want a cut of the action." In the case of a stock, the "action" is price appreciation through earnings growth. When the earnings of a company rise over time, it makes the stock more attractive. As a result, it will attract the attention of additional investors who, in turn, help drive share prices even higher. In addition, higher earnings allow the company to increase the annual dividend to existing shareholders. Dividend increases make the shares even more attractive.

Earnings typically increase as a result of company-specific factors and economic considerations. Company-specific factors include the desirability of the product or service the company offers, the markets it sells into, the quality of the management, and so on. The economic considerations hone in on expected growth in the overall economy as measured by gross domestic product, or GDP. (GDP is the output of all goods and services from the entire country.) As GDP rises, more and more goods and services are being produced. Also, an increasing number of people are finding jobs and receiving raises. These people, in turn, can then afford to purchase more goods and services. So when the economy expands, so do overall corporate earnings. This growth is frequently the result of the Federal Reserve having begun a rate-cutting program many months earlier. After a cycle of interest rate increases, however, the reverse is true. Higher rates typically lead to slower demand. In addition, unemployment rises and corporate earnings growth contracts.

131

And it's because of the importance of interest rates on the ultimate impact on earnings that investors are obsessed with divining the next change of interest rates. Let's face it. Investors have to be fanatical about monitoring interest-rate forecasts, if they want to correctly predict stock-price trends. And since these investors are competing with millions of other investors around the globe, they need to be nimble. They have to anticipate interest-rate actions, not wait for them to be concluded. If they waited until after the Fed completed all of their interest-rate actions, their portfolio would likely be the last to either be helped or hurt by these actions. By correctly forecasting the direction of interest rates, they can buy into the potential benefits of economic expansion, or sell out of the harmful effects of a contracting economy. As a result of this need to anticipate, however, I am convinced that investors have become no better than hyperactive first graders playing musical chairs by one always trying to outanticipate the other.

STOCK SUBSTITUTES AND PRESENT VALUES

An equity investor is concerned about rising and falling interest rates, not only because of how they affect the growth of the economy but also for reasons of substitution and present values. Rising short-term interest rates also usually push up longer-term bond yields. If bond yields rise too much, however, investors begin to consider the possibility of selling their stocks in order to purchase typically less-risky bonds that now offer very attractive yields. They might think, "Hey, if I can get a risk-free return of 6% or so, I'll take it and move back into stocks when the investment outlook for equities looks less uncertain." This "substitution effect," therefore, puts additional pressure on stock prices beyond that of a slowing economy and declining future earnings stream.

Speaking of future streams, that's precisely what equity analysts do when evaluating the intrinsic value of a stock. They use a discounted cash-flow model. First, they estimate the future stream of cash flows that a company will produce. Second, they estimate the current worth of this future stream by discounting the future streams by the current interest rate. The higher the interest rate with which one discounts these future streams, the lower the present value of these streams.

Lastly, interest rates also have a direct impact on companies—particularly those that continuously borrow money by issuing bonds in order to operate and grow. For these debt-heavy companies, higher interest rates will likely cause their interest expense to increase. As they retire old debt at lower interest rates, they will need to take on new debt at higher interest rates. This rising interest expense, which is

133

paid to bond holders, will therefore take an increasingly large chunk out of their overall earnings.

Therefore, the direction of interest rates is extremely important in projecting economic growth, earnings changes, substitutability, and present values—all things analysts and investors look to when forecasting the attractiveness of stocks in general, and sectors in particular. You don't want to ignore, or underestimate, the impact that future interest-rate policy could have on the economy, corporate earnings, and your investments. You want to adjust your portfolios accordingly. In a nutshell, you don't want to fight the Fed!

AN ATYPICAL CHAPTER

Unlike the other rules in this book, this chapter won't give you a step-by-step recipe to develop a portfolio of sectors or industries to be updated once a year or at the end of each month. That's because the Fed doesn't raise or lower rates on a set date annually or semiannually. They step on the gas or press on the brakes when they think the car is going to slow or too fast.

What this chapter will do, however, is help you understand which sectors have typically benefited from or been hurt by rising and falling interest rates. This knowledge is intended to give you the conviction to "stand your ground" by emphasizing cyclical sectors when rates are falling, even if the equity markets don't look as if they are cooperating. Conversely, this knowledge will provide you with the courage to begin thinking about paring back your exposure to equities in general, and cyclical sectors in particular, when interest rates begin to rise.

A DETAILED LOOK AT FED RATE ACTIONS

In order to appreciate market and sector movements on the whole during periods of rising and falling rates, I think it might be helpful to examine the market's reaction to specific rate cycles during the past 50 years. I want to use this as a starting point in order to understand what happens "above the surface" or on the market level, so that we may more fully appreciate what happens "below the surface" when we examine sector performances whenever the Fed begins to raise or lower interest rates.

Take a look at Figure 7.1, which shows the cycles of Fed rate hikes and cuts since 1946. Listed are the rate actions (hikes or cuts) and when the Fed started and ended each cycle, as well as the change in rates. (The discount rate was used from 1946 until February 1989, while the Fed funds rate was used after that.) Finally, it shows the performance of the S&P 500 six and 12 months after the first rate hike or cut.

The last two lines on the table pretty much summarize the whole table, so let's look there first.

FIGURE 7.1

You Typically Don't Want to Ignore the Federal Reserve's Interest Rate Actions

Fed Rate Hikes and Cuts, Interest-Rate Changes, and Stock Market Returns, 1946–2008

Interest-Rate Action	Rate Cycle Periods		Rate Level Change	S&P 500 % Change After First Action	
	Start	End		6 Mos.	12 Mos.
Hike	04/25/46	01/16/53		−20.8%	−22.3%
Cut	**02/05/54**	**04/16/54**		**17.9%**	**41.1%**
Hike	04/15/55	08/23/57		9.1%	26.9%
Cut	**11/15/57**	**04/18/58**		**9.3%**	**34.6%**
Hike	09/12/58	09/11/59		15.9%	18.0%
Cut	**06/10/60**	**08/12/60**		**−2.3%**	**14.9%**
Hike	07/17/63	04/04/69	2.00	8.1%	3.7%
Cut	**11/13/70**	**02/19/71**	**−2.00**	**22.3%**	**9.6%**
Hike	07/16/71	04/25/74	4.00	4.1%	7.6%
Cut	**12/09/74**	**11/22/76**	**−2.75**	**42.3%**	**33.9%**
Hike	08/31/77	02/15/80	7.75	−9.7%	7.4%
Cut	**05/30/80**	**07/28/80**	**−3.00**	**27.4%**	**20.2%**
Hike	09/26/80	05/05/81	4.00	6.5%	−12.4%
Cut	**11/02/81**	**12/15/82**	**−5.50**	**−4.5%**	**9.7%**
Hike	04/09/84	04/09/84	0.50	4.6%	15.1%
Cut	**11/21/84**	**08/21/86**	**−3.50**	**15.6%**	**21.2%**
Hike	09/04/87	02/24/89	1.50	−16.3%	−17.4%
Cut	**07/13/90**	**09/04/92**	**−6.75**	**−13.7%**	**4.1%**
Hike	02/04/94	02/01/95	3.00	−4.0%	−0.4%
Cut	**07/06/95**	**01/31/96**	**−0.75**	**12.7%**	**20.1%**
Hike	03/25/97	03/25/97	0.25	20.9%	41.6%
Cut	**09/29/98**	**11/17/98**	**−0.75**	**22.3%**	**22.3%**
Hike	06/30/99	05/16/00	1.75	8.3%	6.7%
Cut	**01/03/01**	**06/25/03**	**−5.50**	**−3.6%**	**−10.0%**
Hike	06/30/04	06/29/06	4.25	6.8%	5.6%
Cut	**09/18/07**	**09/18/08**	**−4.25**	**−13.5%**	**−20.6%**
		Average for Rate Hikes:	2.50	2.6%	6.2%
		Average for Rate Cuts:	**−3.48**	**10.2%**	**15.5%**

Source: Standard & Poor's, NY Federal Reserve.
Discount Rate used from 1969–1989. Fed funds rate used thereafter.

In general, the Fed typically took more than twice as long to raise rates than to lower them. Rate increases occurred over an average 18-month period. Rate cuts, however, on average happened over a seven-month span. On two occasions the Fed raised rates only once and then stopped, as if saying, "Oops, maybe we shouldn't have done that." We also see that 10 of the 13 rate hikes occurred over a period of more than 11 months. On the other hand, rate cuts usually happened fairly quickly: eight of the 13 rate-cutting cycles were completed in less than eight months.

The Fed usually changed course by starting a rate-cutting cycle an average of eight months after the last rate increase, possibly because the Fed stepped on the brakes a little too hard in the prior rate-tightening cycle. The Fed was a bit slower in raising rates after lowering them, however. In these cases, they waited an average of 12 months. And since we now know that it takes nearly a year before the first rate cut begins to benefit the overall economy, we can see why the Fed took their time before beginning to raise rates once again.

MARKET RETURNS AFTER RATE CHANGES

Now let's review what is of most interest to us: how the market responded to the start of these rate-hiking and rate-cutting cycles. As Figure 7.2 reveals, from 1946 to 2008, the S&P 500's average six-month price rise after the start of each rate-*hiking* cycle was only 2.6%. This abnormally low price advance was likely the result of investors being their old, anticipatory selves. They expected stock prices to suffer from the oncoming rate increases. And 12 months after the first rate hike, the story wasn't too much different. Stock prices rose an average 6.2%, 200 basis points below the longer-term average annual price change. In other words, rate increases, and the prospects of even higher interest rates, have traditionally kept a lid on stock market price advances.

Yet six and 12 months after the Fed started *cutting* interest rates, the S&P 500 soared an average 10.2% and 15.5%, respectively.

FIGURE 7.2

Don't Fight the Fed, in Either Direction!

S&P 500 % Changes After Interest-Rate Hikes and Cuts, 1946–2008

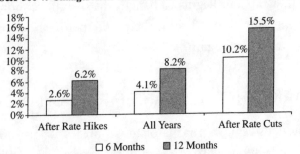

Source: Standard & Poor's Equity Research
Past performance is no guarantee of future results.

FALLING RATES, FLYING PRICES

Consumers love to get two for the price of one. Investors are the same way. As the data shows, Wall Street tends to get very excited whenever the Federal Reserve begins a new rate-cutting program. History shows, but does not guarantee, that when interest rates have started to decline, the S&P 500 has risen in the following six- and 12-month periods by much more than it normally does in six or 12 months. As Figure 7.1 shows, the sharpest six-month price advances came in 1974–1975 and 1980, when the S&P 500 jumped 42.3% and 27.4%, respectively. The highest 12-month advances occurred in 1954 and 1957–1958, when the market soared 41.1% and 34.6%.

IT'S OKAY TO FIGHT THE FED IN
THE SHORT TERM

Since 1946, the Federal Reserve has initiated 13 rate-cutting cycles. Yet not all investors were convinced early on that lower interest rates would help overcome their investment woes. That's because the S&P 500 rose in only eight of these 13-month periods. In other words, the stock market advanced fewer than two of every three times in the six months following the first rate cut. That 62% conviction level is not very encouraging, in my opinion. Clearly many investors were saying, "This time it's different." In fact, as

Figure 7.1 reveals, the S&P 500 fell as much as 13.7% and 13.5% in 1990–1992 and 2007–2008, respectively. I think it is safe to say, therefore, that an investor could have been justified fighting the Fed during the first six months of an interest-rate easing cycle.

BUT DON'T FIGHT THE FED FOR TOO LONG

As Figure 7.1 shows, from 1946 to 2008 the S&P 500 advanced only 62% of the time in the six months following a Fed rate cut. However, it rose 85% of the time in the 12 months after the first rate cut. I believe this statistic is the most compelling for why you don't want to fight the Fed for too long. Eventually the Fed will get it right.

The S&P 500 failed to rise only twice in the 12 months following initial rate cuts: 2001–2002 and 2007–2008. In 2001–2002, the Fed's swift action actually resulted in the shallowest recession since World War II. It failed to save stock prices, however. The U.S. equity markets had to deal with the bursting of the technology bubble, as well as endure the shock of the terrorist attacks domestically on September 11, 2001. These factors contributed to the S&P 500 suffering through the second deepest bear market since WWII. In the 2007–2008 period, the U.S. equity markets had to adjust to the deflation of housing after the housing bubble burst. In addition, markets had to account for the most severe credit crisis since the Panic of 1907.

DIGGING A LITTLE DEEPER

Now that we know that equity prices have typically risen more rapidly than normal after the start of rate reduction cycles, how can we leverage this knowledge from a sector standpoint?

Equity prices as a whole have jumped after initial rate reductions because of the projected beneficial impact on the economy, corporate earnings, substitution, and present values. So, it will probably come as no surprise that the more cyclical, "growth-oriented" sectors have posted superior price performances and outperformed the market more often than the more defensive "value-oriented" sectors during the six and 12 months after the first rate cut.

CYCLICALS LEAD THE WAY

Figure 7.3 shows, in descending order, the average price changes for the 10 sectors in the S&P 500 in a 12-month period after the Fed started a rate-cutting program since 1946. The table also shows how frequently these sectors beat the S&P 500 during these 13 rate-cutting periods.

One note of clarification: S&P sector–level data goes back to 1990. Prior to 1990, only industry indexes existed. The data in Figure 7.3 show the average sector-level results from 1990 to 2008. Prior to that, I used the average price changes for the underlying industries. And since I didn't

FIGURE 7.3

Aim for "Cyclical" Sectors After Rate Cuts

Sector Performances and Frequencies of Beating the Market
12 Months After the First Rate Cut, 1946–2008

S&P 500 Sectors	Average % Change	Frequency of Beating S&P 500
Information Technology	28%	77%
Consumer Discretionary	27%	69%
Industrials	24%	69%
Consumer Staples	23%	77%
Health Care	21%	62%
Average of All Sectors/Industries	**19%**	**53%**
Financial	17%	54%
Materials	14%	38%
Energy	11%	31%
Telecommunications Services	5%	17%
Utilities	5%	15%

Source: Standard & Poor's Equity Research
Past performance is no guarantee of future results.

want to perpetuate an "oranges-to-tangerines" comparison by showing the average price change for the S&P 500 during these periods, I show the average return for all sectors and their underlying industries.

Twelve months after the first rate cut, investors' interest in cyclical sectors has been pronounced. The Consumer Discretionary, Industrials, and Information Technology sectors have posted superior average price gains. In addition, they have shown above-average frequencies of beating the overall market. The average sector/industry has posted an average annual return of 19%, which is more than twice the average annual increase of 8.2% for the S&P 500 since World War II. In addition, the average sector/industry has beaten the S&P 500 53% of the time. Yet these three sectors have recorded price gains in excess of 24% each. What's more, each of them has beaten the S&P 500 at least two out of every three times.

SURPRISING STRENGTH

Consumer Staples and Health Care have also posted above-average returns and frequencies of beating the S&P 500. Initially I was surprised by this strength, since these groups are traditionally regarded as defensive. That's because the demand for their products and services is fairly static. This strong showing by Consumer Staples and Health Care may be due to the reluctance of investors to dive into cyclical equities with both feet. Many probably prefer to hedge their bets in case the economy and stock market do not respond so favorably to interest-rate cuts.

WEEDING OUT THE WEAKLINGS

The pronounced underperformers 12 months after the first rate cut were the Energy, Materials, and Utilities sectors, which gained between 5% and 14% and recorded frequencies of beating the S&P 500 that were anywhere from a high of 38% to a low of 15%. The Energy and Materials sectors possibly lagged the overall market since they were the groups that had already seen their day in the sun. These two groups historically have done well during the latter stages of a prior economic expansion. Investors have traditionally gravitated toward "real-asset" sectors as inflation has crept higher. Once the Fed started cutting rates, however, investors likely engaged in a bit of sector rotation. They shifted away from those areas of waning strength and toward those that were projected to do better. Utilities likely lagged the market as these income-oriented issues were bypassed in favor of higher-octane groups.

144

I purposely avoided talking about the results for the Telecommunications Services sector, since this group has been around only since the late 1980s. As a result, it does not have enough history under its belt, in my opinion, to make their average results a helpful guide to possible future performance. This might be a good time to remind you that I don't think history is ever gospel, but I do believe it makes a pretty good guide.

HIGHER RATES, LOWER AVERAGE ADVANCES

Too much of anything is not good, however, especially if it has to do with partying. After a series of interest-rate cuts, the economy and stock market have typically been partying! So it's the Federal Reserve's responsibility to bring this party to an end. The Fed attempts to do this in a controlled fashion by taking away the punch bowl through a gradual rise in short-term interest rates. But because investors have long memories, they tend to recall the unfavorable outcome of prior attempts by the Fed to slow the growth in the overall economy. In short, investors remember that the Fed tends to overdo things. As a result, investors begin to worry that the Fed will once again press too hard on the economic brakes.

As Figure 7.2 reminds us, once the Fed starts hiking interest rates, the market's returns suffer, over both a six- and 12-month timeframe. The 2.6% six-month rise and 6.2% average 12-month advance were each less than what the S&P 500 has typically recorded in all six- and 12-month periods since 1946. I guess the only good thing that can be said about the market's performance after rate increases is that at least they have been positive. Also, as Figure 7.1 shows, the S&P 500 has declined only 31% of the time both six and 12 months after the Fed has started raising rates, which is encouraging. I guess some partygoers never want to give up!

SECTOR STANDOUTS AND SLACKERS

Figure 7.4 shows the average price change and frequency of beating the S&P 500 six and 12 months after the Fed

FIGURE 7.4

Aiming for More "Defensive" Sectors After Rate Hikes

Sector Performances and Frequencies of Beating the Market
12 Months After the First Rate Hike, 1946–2008

S&P 500 Sectors	Average % Change	Frequency of Beating S&P 500
Information Technology	20%	69%
Health Care	13%	54%
Telecommunications Services	10%	67%
Energy	10%	46%
Average of All Sectors/Industries	**9%**	**44%**
Consumer Staples	7%	46%
Industrials	7%	23%
Consumer Discretionary	7%	38%
Utilities	5%	38%
Financial	4%	38%
Materials	3%	31%

Source: Standard & Poor's Equity Research
Past performance is no guarantee of future results.

has started *raising* interest rates. The data is sorted in descending order by average percent change.

Historical sector performances 12 months after the first rate hike offer less helpful or convincing investment guidance, in my opinion, than they did after the first rate cut. They tell a less clear story this time around as to which sectors are typically helped or hurt by rising rates. Is it because investors don't believe that the party is really ending? Could it be similar to the frequent admonition "all congressmen are ineffectual—except my own," meaning that while other stocks may get hurt, mine won't? Or is it because the reasons behind the Fed beginning to raise rates are more varied than the reasons to lower them? The truth could contain a little of each.

At first, I would have expected to see a reverse listing of winners and losers after rate hikes than after rate cuts. This apparently was not the case. I have studied all bear markets since 1945. (A bear market is defined as an S&P 500 price decline of 20% or more from the peak of the prior bull market.) In a bear market, there typically is no place to hide, as all 10 sectors post average price declines. The lowest price declines, however, have historically come from the Consumer Staples, Health Care, and Utilities sectors. That's because in good times and bad, people still eat, drink, smoke, get sick, and heat their homes. As a result, I frequently say that "when the going gets tough, the tough go eating, smoking, and drinking. And if they overdo it, they go to the doctor." As a result of my prior work with bear markets, I thought I would see the likes of Information Technology on the bottom and Utilities on the top. Obviously, I was mistaken.

My assumption is no doubt incorrect for two reasons. First, remember that investors are always anticipating events. Since the Fed typically begins raising rates an average

12 months after their last rate cut, maybe investors have rotated into those sectors that are expected to be shielded from the effects of rising rates well before the first rate hike.

Another reason could be that in a rising-rate environment, one has to be aware of the impact not only on the overall economy but also on the specific industries and companies.

WHY TECH WAS ON TOP

Information Technology stocks have done well after initial rate hikes for two possible reasons. First, investors may rationalize that as the economy will likely slow because of rising interest rates, companies may begin to spend more on technology in order to improve productivity. They figure that these companies will want to remain price competitive during a potential slump in orders. Rather than hire more employees as the economy slows, it is reasoned, companies will provide the existing workers with better technology.

Another reason Information Technology companies have continued to post strong price gains after the Fed has started raising interest rates could be that most technology companies have little debt on their balance sheets. As a result, because these firms don't frequently borrow money in order to operate, their interest expense will not go up as interest rates rise. This situation will help their earnings growth on a relative basis.

Utilities, on the other hand, are big users of debt and typically feel the pinch of higher interest rates on their overall earnings. So, investors may shy away from these big borrowers. In addition, many investors who own Utilities do so for their dividend yield. As a result, Utilities are frequently referred to as "bond substitutes, or proxies." Utilities, therefore, may feel the effects of "substitution" more acutely than do other sectors.

In conclusion, the data show that investors aren't very sure where to turn when interest rates are on the rise. While some defensive sectors, such as Health Care, have held up well, others, such as Utilities, have not. And although some cyclical sectors, such as Financials, have taken it on the chin as interest rates have begun to rise, others, such as Information Technology, have not because of the absence of interest expense.

TAKEAWAYS

As I said earlier, this is an atypical chapter. Unlike the other rules in this book, this chapter won't give you a step-by-step recipe to develop a portfolio of sectors or industries to be updated once a year or at the end of each month. That's because the Fed doesn't raise or lower rates on a set date annually or semiannually. They step on the gas or press on the brakes when they think the car is going to slow or too fast.

What this chapter did do, I hope, was help you understand how the S&P 500 has been affected by rising and falling interest rates. It should help you gain the conviction to "stand your ground" when rates are falling yet pare back your exposure to equities if the party is still going strong, even though the punch bowl is long gone.

As you have seen in the resulting data, the response by sectors within the S&P 500 has not been overly consistent, particularly when the Fed starts raising rates. I think this reaction is mainly the result of trying to put too much faith in one indicator, namely, interest rates. While I still believe the direction of interest rates is the most important criterion in evaluating the direction of equity prices, it is by no means the only one. Many times the direction of sector prices may be influenced by the concentration of more minor, sector-specific factors.

I am more encouraged by the magnitude of sector price returns and frequencies of beating the market after the beginning of rate cuts than I am after the start of rate hikes. In my opinion, the data provide convincing evidence that a move back into equities, particularly into cyclical groups, is more in order after a rate cut than after a hike. That doesn't mean that the data surrounding sector returns after the start of a new rate-hiking cycle is unhelpful. On the contrary, I think the data show that investors are well advised to tread very carefully after a rate hike, as stocks in general haven't performed up to par at that time. And from a sector standpoint, I advise you not to assume automatically that those sectors that went up the most when interest rates fell will be the ones to go down the most when interest rates rise.

If things were that easy, would you need to buy any book on investing?

The envelope, please.

—ACADEMY AWARD PRESENTER

SUMMARY

Ranking the Rules

Whenever I'm on TV, I frequently get asked, "If you could own just one stock, what would it be?" It's interesting that people want to narrow the options down to just one. Which is your favorite movie, song, or athlete? What's the one thing you would do to change your life? I guess people search for "one" because it is a fairly simple number to deal with and the decision is made for you. But didn't Three Dog Night sing "One is the loneliest number"? Oh well, I guess that's just human nature.

After I present the "Seven Rules of Wall Street" to a group of investors, at least one audience member will ask, "Which one do you like best?" Ah, an interesting question! And yes, I will give you my answer. But before revealing the "winner" (shades of the Miss America Contest!), let's take another look at the contestants and compare their performances.

Figure S.1 shows the performances (average annual return and compound annual growth rate), risks (standard

FIGURE S.1

Ranking the Rules: Performances in the 17 Years from 1991 to 2007

Performances Data for the Rules, 1991–2007					
The Rules of Wall Street	Average Annual Return	Compound Growth Rate	Standard Deviation	Risk-Adjusted Return	Frequency of Beating S&P 500
S&P 500	**10.4%**	**9.2%**	**16.5**	**0.63**	**NA**
Let Your Winners Ride					
Industries	20.4%	17.7%	24.9	0.82	76%
Cap-Weighted Sectors	12.7%	10.8%	20.6	0.62	71%
Equally Weighted Sectors	13.8%	13.0%	18.7	0.74	76%
As Goes January					
Industries	19.9%	17.0%	27.6	0.72	65%
Cap-Weighted Sectors	14.7%	12.8%	21.0	0.70	76%
Equally Weighted Sectors	16.7%	15.2%	18.6	0.90	76%
Sell in May (Health Care)					
Cap-Weighted Sectors	12.2%	11.5%	17.1	0.71	65%
Equally Weighted Sectors	13.0%	12.4%	14.2	0.92	67%
No Free Lunch					
Cap-Weighted Sectors	13.2%	11.5%	19.7	0.67	53%
Equally Weighted Sectors	14.6%	13.0%	19.3	0.76	65%
There's Always a Bull Market Someplace					
Industries	22.4%	20.3%	24.0	0.93	71%
Cap-Weighted Sectors	14.6%	13.7%	16.5	0.88	76%
Equally Weighted Sectors	17.2%	16.5%	13.7	1.26	71%

Source: Standard & Poor's Equity Research
Past performance is no guarantee of future results.

deviation and risk-adjusted return), and frequency of market outperformance for six of the seven rules.

I left out Rule 7, Don't Fight the Fed, as it does not lend itself easily to the composition and maintenance of a portfolio that is updated on a monthly, semiannual, or annual basis. Therefore, I will stick with six: Let Your Winners Ride, As Goes January, Sell in May, No Free Lunch, and There's Always a Bull Market Someplace.

Did you count only five? Very good! That's because I took each of the five rules and added an additional look, using Rule 6, Don't Get Mad—Get Even, to see how an equally weighted approach adds octane to each of these market-cap-weighted rules.

THREE MINIMUM REQUIREMENTS

Before examining each rule, I want to share with you the three things I look for when determining if a discipline is worth embracing. First, the compound growth rate needs to be at least 300 basis points (3 percentage points) higher than that for the S&P 500. If a discipline offers less, I question whether it is worth my time.

Second, the risk-adjusted return has to be higher than that for the S&P 500. If not, why bother? Why eke out a higher return only to have to suffer through gut-wrenching swings in monthly and annual price changes?

Lastly, I need a frequency of market outperformance that is at least 67% (meaning this discipline beats the market three out of every four times). If it is lower than 67%, I would not be able to endure the frequent subpar performances in the hope of scoring the infrequent "big payoff." Let's face it, because of my low risk–tolerance level (remember, I am indecisive, impatient, and emotional), I don't think I could stick with a discipline where I would have to wait until locusts rehatch before I beat the market again.

ONE POINT OF CLARIFICATION

The data in the table may look a bit different than what was shown in previous chapters. That's because some data in earlier chapters started in 1945, while others started in 1970, 1990, or 1991. Therefore, in an effort to make more meaningful "apples-to-apples" comparisons, I recalculated and displayed the returns, risk, and frequencies of market outperformance from a time period that was consistent to all: 1991 to 2007.

So now, let's go through each rule, getting my take on each one's track record and likelihood of future outperformance.

LET YOUR WINNERS RIDE

The good thing about the Let Your Winners Ride rule is that it forces an investor not to give up on a winning industry or sector too soon. You may believe an investment has run too far—to either the upside or the downside—only to be proven wrong. Frequently, trends last a lot longer than most people think they will. Therefore this rule is a good one to help stick with, or continue to avoid, sectors or industries.

I love the performance of this rule on an industry level—850 basis points of annual outperformance on a compound growth basis, a superior risk-adjusted return, and a whopping 76% frequency of market outperformance. Who can complain?

Well, actually I can. One problem—as I have already mentioned a few times—is that you can't buy industry-level ETFs. You have to use an individual stock as an industry's proxy. That requires me to make a decision, and you know how I feel about doing that.

Another problem is that because you are locking yourself into a portfolio for a full year, you may be experiencing another investing shortcoming: commitment to a stock for an extended period of time. When I commit this way, I worry that I may be buying the portfolio just as it is about to lose its momentum. If you are like I am, maybe this approach isn't the best one for you.

Using sector ETFs to invest in the Let Your Winners Ride rule is comparatively easy, but the performance is nowhere near as good as on an industry level. In fact, its margin of outperformance is below my threshold. The risk-adjusted return is okay (at least it's better than the market) and the frequency of market outperformance is eye-catching at 71%. Yet I just keep coming back to the paltry relative return. It reminds me of when I am having dinner with a friend and we order the same dish—only to find that my portion is smaller than his. I keep hoping for more.

And by embracing an equally weighted sector ETF approach, I have gotten more—a margin of outperformance that is back above the 300 basis-point threshold, while experiencing a lower standard deviation and higher risk-adjusted return. What's more, my frequency of market outperformance has jumped back up to 76%. Not bad. Of the three, I prefer the equally weighted approach, as the simplicity makes up for the higher return of investing on an industry level.

AS GOES JANUARY

Right off the bat I can say that the average margin of market outperformance is sufficient for all three versions of this rule—industry, market-cap-weighted sectors, and equally weighted sectors. The risk-adjusted returns are also better than that for the S&P 500.

So far, so good.

On the industry level, however, the frequency of market outperformance falls a bit short. I think 65% is too infrequent for me. Call me spoiled, but I'd prefer to get an outperformance level that is above 70%.

The worry that I had about buying into a group that was just about to head lower with the Let Your Winners Ride portfolio is satisfied by the As Goes January rule, since it looks at the most recent month's performance alone. However, it introduces another concern: do I really want to commit myself to a stock for a year based solely on one month's day in the sun? What if it ended up being a false breakout and proceeded to tank for the remainder of the year? I guess that's the jaded New Yorker in me. But it makes sense. Other than Hollywood movie stars, who gets married after only a one-month fling?

159

If I did select this rule, again I would probably lean toward the equally weighted sector approach. It shows a strong margin of market outperformance, it has a relatively low volatility, and hence has a higher risk-adjusted return. And who wouldn't be happy with a 76% (greater than three out of four) frequency of market outperformance?

Should I stop here? Okay, I'll keep going.

SELL IN MAY

Let's cut to the chase. The Sell in May rule is cute, but it better serves as an interesting investment article to publish in early May than as a rule to live and invest by. Of course, it does serve to remind us that the summer months can be a bit challenging for equity investors, so I guess it does have its purposes.

Don't get me wrong. If I thought it was a bad rule, I wouldn't have included it in the book. I'm just saying that if I had to choose one rule that gives me the overall performance I want, as well as the conviction that it will continue to work going forward, this would not be it.

What's more, on a market-cap-weighted sector level, the margin of annual outperformance doesn't cut it, nor does the frequency of market outperformance. On an equally weighted basis, however, I can squeeze out a satisfactory level of annual returns. Yet the frequency of annual market outperformance doesn't really improve all that much, so I will chalk up this rule as one of academic interest.

NO FREE LUNCH

For someone who desires as little involvement with their portfolio as possible, short of buying into a Target Date mutual fund, this could be the best rule in the book. But I must say that, like the Sell in May rule, this one also has its shortcomings.

On a market-cap-weighted basis, the marginal excess return is minimal, and the risk-adjusted return is only slightly better than that for the S&P 500. And since we are casting stones, the frequency of market performance is pretty poor as well, at only 53% (see Figure S.1). Of all of the rules, I would say that in the 17-year period evaluated, this rule is the least impressive.

In order to make this rule appear worthy of entry into this book, you have to venture into the equally weighted sector arena. There I received the more than 300 basis points of marginal outperformance that I desire. I was also able to get a risk-adjusted return that was superior enough to the S&P 500's to make me think it was not a statistical anomaly. Yet I was not all that impressed with the frequency with which this rule beat the market at only 65%.

On the other hand, its lackluster overall performance has helped me make a decision as to my favorite rule in the book.

161

THERE'S ALWAYS A BULL MARKET SOMEPLACE

On an industry level, both the average annual return and compound annual growth rate were the highest of all rules. In both cases, the margin of annual outperformance was in excess of 1,100 basis points, or more than 11 full percentage points per year. Plus, it offered the second-highest risk-adjusted return and beat the market more than 70% of the time. Satisfaction abounds!

But I'm not all that surprised about these statistics, since my Industry Momentum portfolio has been delivering similar performance results to individual investors from our www.spoutlook.com Web site and to financial advisors from www.advisorinsight.com since April 1999.

Concerns? Yes, there are two. First, as with the Let Your Winners Ride and As Goes January rules, there are no industry-level ETFs. You've got to select the proxy stocks. Second, at 300%, the turnover is fairly high. Therefore this rule is best employed with a discount broker in a tax-deferred environment.

On a market-cap-weighted sector level, you give up a lot of performance in order to gain simplicity. The margin of outperformance slips to 450 basis points from 1,100, and the risk-adjusted return dipped below 0.90. Still, the frequency of market outperformance did rise to 76%, the highest level of outperformance recorded and accomplished by only four other portfolios.

AND THE WINNER IS …

Of all 13 portfolios, the one I favor most is There's Always a Bull Market Someplace, which uses equally weighted S&P 500 sectors. It has all of the right statistics: a compound annual growth rate that exceeded the S&P 500's by more than 700 basis points; a standard deviation of 13.7, which is nearly 300 basis points below that of the market's 16.5; and a risk-adjusted return that topped 1.00 at a whopping 1.26! Finally, it offered an average frequency of annual outperformance that exceeded 70%.

Even more encouraging is that this portfolio allows an investor to evaluate and adjust his or her portfolio every month, so no one, including me, has to overcome the fear of commitment for an extended period of time. Plus, because it uses ETFs, it's an incredibly easy rule to follow. Finally, the annual turnover—while still relatively high at 180%—is still a lot better than the 225% for the market-cap-weighted sector portfolio and the 300% for the industry portfolio.

So, there you have it: the rules, the results, and the winner. As with all things in life, feel free to disagree with my assessments and my final selection. I am fully aware that everyone has a different approach to investing. A discipline that sounds appropriate to one person, may appear illogical to another. Therefore, I encourage you to select the rule that feels best to you. Good luck!

GLOSSARY

No doubt some investment terminology used throughout this book is unfamiliar to you. The terms below are the prominent ones that have appeared in the previous chapters. By its nature, a glossary like this cannot be comprehensive. For a more complete listing of financial terms, I recommend *A Dictionary of Finance and Investment Terms,* by John Downes and Jordan Elliot Goodman (Barron's). I refer to it frequently.

Average Annual Return.   The simple arithmetic mean price change over a specified period of time. It is computed by summing all data items and then dividing by the count of the data items. For example, a 50% decline in one year and a 50% advance in the following year would give a simple mean average return of 0% (50 − 50/2 = 0). The average annual return is usually higher than the compound annual growth rate, where a 50% decline requires a 100% rise to break even. For example, if you had $10,000 in your portfolio and it declined by 50%, you would be left with $5,000. You would therefore need a 100% gain to get back to your $10,000 original value.

Basis Point.   One-one hundredth of a percentage point. Interest rates are typically displayed out to two decimal places, such as 4.25%. It's easier to say "basis points" than it is "one hundredths of a percentage point," but they mean the same thing. The difference between 4.25% and 4.00% is 25 basis points, or 25/100ths of a percentage point.

Beta.   A relative measure of volatility. It shows how much a stock fluctuates in comparison with a broader benchmark. A reading of 1.0 means that a stock's volatility is equal to that of the S&P 500. A beta that is higher than 1.0 reflects higher relative volatility. A beta below 1.0 reflects lower relative volatility.

Cash Flow.   Net income (sales/revenues minus operating expenses) adding back amortization and depreciation expenses. In a formula, it would look like this: Net Income + Amortization/Depreciation. Free cash flow goes one step further by subtracting two additional items: capital expenditures and changes in working capital. Free cash flow attempts to remove accounting tricks that could hide the true cash-generating ability of a company.

Compound Annual Growth Rate.   The return a portfolio would experience over a particular time period by including the effects of compounding both increases and decreases. See *Average Annual Return* for examples of differing results.

Discount Rate. The rate the Federal Reserve would charge a Fed member bank for overnight loans in order to meet reserve requirements. Banks would rather borrow from one another than go to the Fed. Prior to 1989, the Federal Reserve would announce changes to the discount rate but not to the Fed funds rate. Fed watchers would have to estimate when the Fed funds rate was raised or lowered. In an effort to offer increased transparency of Federal Open Market Committee (FOMC) actions, Fed chairman Alan Greenspan began announcing Fed funds rate changes in 1989.

Equally Weighted Index. All companies within an index are weighted equally. Each company exerts the same influence on the performance of the index. Market capitalization is meaningless. Within the S&P 500, each company has a 0.20% representation, or weighting.

Fed Funds Rate. The rate member banks of the Federal Reserve System charge one another for overnight loans, in order to meet reserve requirements. Banks would rather borrow from one another than from the Fed, just as siblings would rather ask for loans from one another before going to Mom or Dad for a loan. Prior to 1989, the Federal Reserve would announce changes to the discount rate but not to the Fed funds rate. Fed watchers would have to estimate when the Fed funds rate was raised or lowered. In an effort to offer increased transparency of Federal Open Market Committee

(FOMC) actions, Fed chairman Alan Greenspan began announcing Fed funds rate changes in 1989.

Frequency of Beating the S&P 500 (or market). The percentage of the observations (usually years) in which the portfolio, sector, or industry has outperformed its benchmark, usually the S&P 500 index, also known as "the market."

Fundamentally Weighted Indexes. A company's representation in an index is based on a metric of its fundamental valuations. Factors that could be considered include dividend yield or price-to-earnings ratios (P/Es). Each ETF creator may have its own way of deciding which fundamentals are most important. For example, Wisdom Tree offers a fundamentally weighted family of ETFs.

Gross Domestic Product (GDP). The output of all goods and services produced in one country. The means of production may emanate from either foreign- or domestically owned companies. If they are produced on U.S. soil, then they are counted in the U.S. GDP.

Industry. A grouping of companies that provide similar products or services. The 500 companies in the S&P 500 are assigned to approximately 130 industries.

Large-Cap Stocks. Stocks with market capitalizations above $4.0 billion.

Market Capitalization. The number of common shares outstanding times the share price. Also called "market cap." Large-cap companies typically have market capitalizations in excess of $4.0 billion. Small-cap stocks have market caps below $1.5 billion. Mid-cap stocks have market capitalizations between $1.5 billion and $4.0 billion. These thresholds are not universally agreed upon.

Market-Capitalization-Weighted Index. A company's proportion of the index is based upon its market capitalization. The larger the market cap, the greater the influence it has on the performance of the index.

Market Value. See *Market Capitalization*. The term "market value" is synonymous with market cap.

169

Mean. A simple average (the sum of data items divided by the count of data items).

Median. The midpoint in a series of values. This form of average helps remove the distortions from extreme highs and lows.

Mid-Cap Stocks. Stocks that have market capitalizations between $1.5 billion and $4.0 billion.

Price-Weighted Indexes. A stock's representation within an index is based on its price. The level of the index is determined by summing the prices of all component companies and dividing by the number of companies in the index.

Thus, the higher-priced stock has the greater influence on the performance of the index. The Dow Jones Industrial Average (DJIA) is price-weighted.

Risk. See *Standard Deviation*.

Sector. A grouping of industries whose earnings and share price action are affected by similar macro- and microeconomic events as well as legislative or regulatory actions. The nearly 130 industries are grouped into 10 sectors. They are Consumer Discretionary, Consumer Staples, Energy, Financials, Health Care, Industrials, Information Technology, Materials, Telecommunications Services, and Utilities.

Small-Cap Stocks. Stocks that have market capitalizations below $1.5 billion.

Standard Deviation. A statistical measure of how much a data point deviates from the standard or average. It is used to spot extremes, since two-thirds of all observations fall within one standard deviation from the mean, and 92% of all observations fall within two standard deviations. Anything beyond two standard deviations is a true extreme.

Turnover. The amount by which holdings (stocks, industries, or sectors) in a portfolio have been replaced within a year. In a 20-stock portfolio, a 100% turnover indicates that 20 stocks have been bought and sold during the year. Turnover is correlated with cost of transaction, tax consequences, and amount of end-of-year paperwork.

INDEX

Index

Index

Index